THE

NUMEROLOGY

HANDBOOK

TANIA GABRIELLE

THE
NUMEROLOGY
HANDBOOK

UNCOVER YOUR DESTINY
AND MANIFEST YOUR FUTURE
WITH THE POWER OF
NUMBERS

FAIR WINDS

First Published in 2019 by Fair Winds Press, an imprint of The Quarto Group, 100 Cummings Center, Suite 265-D, Beverly, MA 01915, USA.
T (978) 282-9590 F (978) 283-2742 QuartoKnows.com

Fair Winds Press titles are also available at discount for retail, wholesale, promotional, and bulk purchase. For details, contact the Special Sales Manager by email at specialsales@quarto.com or by mail at The Quarto Group, Attn: Special Sales Manager, 100 Cummings Center, Suite 265-D, Beverly, MA 01915, USA.

23 22 21 20 19   1 2 3 4 5

ISBN: 978-1-59233-874-0

Digital edition published in 2019
Library of Congress Cataloging-in-Publication Data available
The content for this book was previously published in *The Ultimate Guide to Numerology* by Tania Gabrielle (Fair Winds Press, 2018).

Cover Design: Landers Miller Design
Interior Design and Page Layout: Sporto
Illustration: Landers Miller Design

Printed in China

The information in this book is for educational purposes only. It is not intended to replace the advice of a physician or medical practitioner. Please see your health-care provider before beginning any new health program.

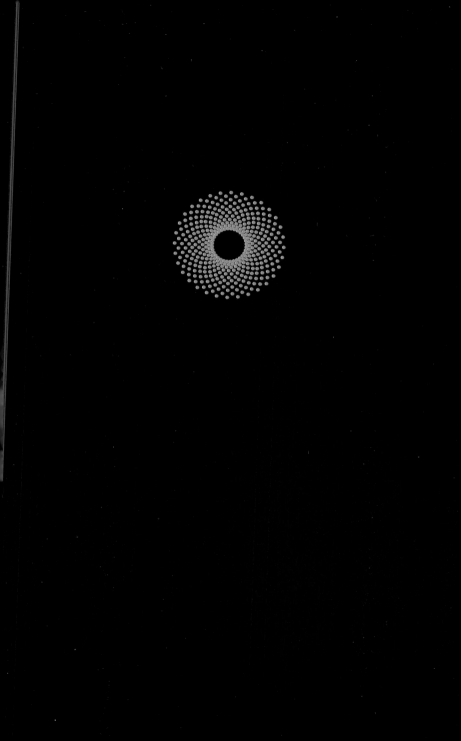

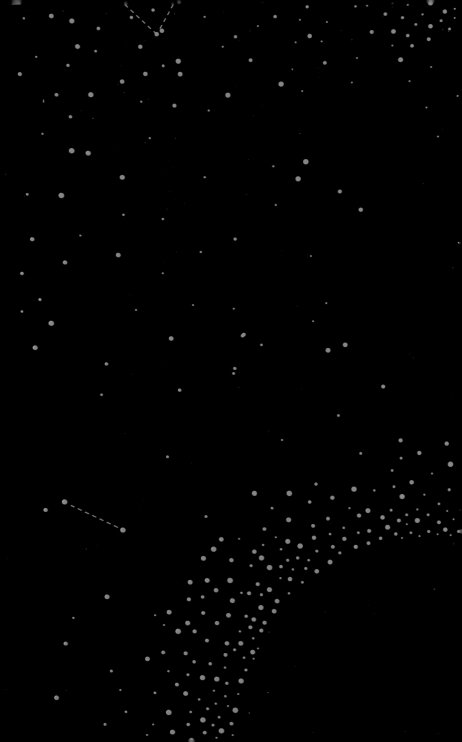

CONTENTS

CHAPTER 1:
Your Birthday Code • **9**

CHAPTER 2:
Your Birth Name Code • **19**

CHAPTER 3:
Single Digits 1–9 and the Three Triads • **33**

CHAPTER 4:
Master Numbers 11–99 • **71**

CHAPTER 5:
Double Digit Numbers 10–98 • **89**

CHAPTER 6:
Personal Year, Month, and Days
and Your Power Cycles • **129**

CHAPTER 7:
Meaning of Your Personal Cycles • **141**

CHAPTER 8:
Address Numbers • **155**

ACKNOWLEDGMENTS • **170**

ABOUT THE AUTHOR • **171**

INDEX • **172**

CHAPTER 1

YOUR BIRTHDAY CODE

ON THE DAY YOU WERE BORN, YOU ACTIVATED A MAGNIFICENT BIRTH CODE. This Birth Code is the blueprint to your soul, the translation of your soul contract for this lifetime. Numerology, the science of the meaning of numbers, is designed to translate the Blueprint of your Soul to reveal your spiritual contract. This book will give you the keys.

Numbers are a gateway into developing your intuition. When you first meet someone, you may have a gut feeling about him or her. Having access to numbers gives you another perspective on their soul and permission to confirm what you already felt intuitively.

Everything is energy. Everything carries a vibrational force. Every number is a unique vibration with a profound meaning. All the numbers aligned within one person, entity, or family, create a code. Each sector of a code contributes to a symphony of vibrant frequencies that make up all the interconnections of your life.

Numbers are the essence of how life expresses itself. In understanding your Birth Code, you will discover who you truly are at soul level, how to use your special gifts, and how you overcome obstacles to gain the wisdom and courage to fulfill your divine mission.

The Three Important Numbers in your Birth Code

You have many numbers in your birthday and birth certificate name. However, there are three numbers that impact you the most. Throughout this manual, they will be referred to as the Three Important Numbers in your Birth Code.

Your unique Birth Code is made up of:

1. Your Day of Birth Number—the Day of the Month you were born

2. Your Life Purpose Number—the total sum of your full birth Date

3. Your Destiny Number—the total sum of letters in your birth certificate name (see Chapter 2)

Combined into a powerful triad, your Birth Code is a spiritual and practical formula that is totally unique to you.

Your Birth Code unlocks the secrets of your birth promise—special gifts, talents, your personality, the nature of your mission, and corresponding lessons. Each of your three individual personal frequencies describes how you think, feel, act, and experience life. They form the basic building blocks that make up your Divine DNA code.

Let's discover the first two important numbers in your Birth Code, beginning with your Day of Birth Number—the easiest to calculate!

Your DAY of BIRTH Number

Every person and entity (like a business, product launch, live event, ceremony, first meeting) is born on a specific day of the month. The Day of Birth Number gives you instant insights into someone's natural disposition, their way of being and tendencies, who they are day-to-day, moment-to-moment—even if you do not know their age. This allows you to do a quick reading on anyone if you know they were born on the 5th, 22nd, or 17th, etc.—so, regardless of whether you know their year of birth or not, you can read this part of their birth code.

WHAT IS YOUR DAY OF BIRTH NUMBER?

If you were born on the first through the ninth of any month, your Day of Birth corresponds to that number. If

you are born between the tenth through the thirty-first of any month, you will be impacted by one additional double-digit number (sometimes two) along with the single digit or "root number." Find the root number by adding together the digits of your Day of Birth (twice, if the result is another double-digit number). Read the descriptions in Chapters 4 and 5 for your Day of Birth Number and your root number(s).

IF YOU WERE BORN ON THE:	YOUR DAY OF BIRTH IS:	THE ROOT NUMBER IS:	AND THE ROOT NUMBER IS:
1ST	1		
2ND	2		
3RD	3		
4TH	4		
5TH	5		
6TH	6		
7TH	7		
8TH	8		
9TH	9		
10TH	10	$1 + 0 = 1$	
11TH	11	$1 + 1 = 2$	
12TH	12	$1 + 2 = 3$	
13TH	13	$1 + 3 = 4$	
14TH	14	$1 + 4 = 5$	
15TH	15	$1 + 5 = 6$	
16TH	16	$1 + 6 = 7$	
17TH	17	$1 + 7 = 8$	

(continued)

IF YOU WERE BORN ON THE:	YOUR DAY OF BIRTH IS:	THE ROOT NUMBER IS:		AND THE ROOT NUMBER IS:
18TH	18	1 + 8 = 9		
19TH	19	1 + 9 = 10	→	1 + 0 = 1
20TH	20	2 + 0 = 2		
21ST	21	2 + 1 = 3		
22ND	22	2 + 2 = 4		
23RD	23	2 + 3 = 5		
24TH	24	2 + 4 = 6		
25TH	25	2 + 5 = 7		
26TH	26	2 + 6 = 8		
27TH	27	2 + 7 = 9		
28TH	28	2 + 8 = 10	→	1 + 0 = 1
29TH	29	2 + 9 = 11	→	1 + 1 = 2
30TH	30	3 + 0 = 3		
31ST	31	3 + 1 = 4		

Your LIFE PURPOSE Number

Adding all the digits in a given birthday results in the Life Purpose Number, one of the Three Important Numbers in your Birth Code.

Your Life Purpose is a powerful frequency revealing how you need to express your soul purpose: What is the main reason you are here? What is your main lesson? How are you uniquely designed to feel happily engaged with our life? What qualities will help you manifest the most success?

Once you calculate your Life Purpose Number you'll hold the keys to your unique purpose for being here on Earth in this lifetime.

WHAT IS YOUR LIFE PURPOSE NUMBER?

The Life Purpose Number is derived by adding each single digit in a person's full birthday. If it's two digits, it must then be reduced (sometimes twice) to its single-digit "root" number. (Hint: Anyone who is born in the 1900s will automatically have a two-digit Life Purpose Number). See Chapter 5 to discover the meaning of all two-digit numbers (except "master numbers" 11, 22, 33, 44). See Chapter 3 to discover the meaning of all nine single digit numbers.

MONTH		DAY		YEAR		LIFE PURPOSE NUMBER
1–12	+	1–31	+	xxxx	=	?

MAY		10		1972		LIFE PURPOSE NUMBER
5	+	1 + 0	+	1 + 9 + 7 + 2	=	**25** COMPOUND LIFE PURPOSE NUMBER
						2 + 5 = **7** ROOT LIFE PURPOSE

This person has a 25 / 7 Life Purpose Number.

If a person's Life Purpose Number (full birthday) adds up to **19, 28, 29, 37, 38, 39, 46, 47,** or **48**, then you must add two times before you arrive at the single digit root number. Read the descriptions of all three numbers for the full picture.

Another example:

SEPTEMBER		16		1984		COMPOUND LIFE PURPOSE NUMBER
9	+	1 + 6	+	1 + 9 + 8 + 4	=	**38** (3 + 8 = **11**)
						1 + 1 = **2** ROOT LIFE PURPOSE

Let's look at four examples. Case Studies 3 and 4 are examples of birthdays that require *two* calculations and result in a Life Purpose made up of three separate numbers.

CASE STUDY 1: Justin Timberlake

Justin Timberlake was born on January 31, 1981.

JANUARY		31		1981		COMPOUND LIFE PURPOSE NUMBER
1	+	3 + 1	+	1 + 9 + 8 + 1	=	**24**
						2 + 4 = **6** ROOT LIFE PURPOSE

CASE STUDY 2: Mariel Hemingway

Mariel Hemingway was born on November 22, 1961.

NOVEMBER		22		1961		COMPOUND LIFE PURPOSE NUMBER
1 + 1	+	2 + 2	+	1 + 9 + 6 + 1	=	**23**
						2 + 3 = **5** ROOT LIFE PURPOSE

CASE STUDY 3: Tony Robbins

Tony Robbins was born on February 29, 1960.

FEBRUARY		29		1960		COMPOUND LIFE PURPOSE NUMBER
2	+	2 + 9	+	1 + 9 + 6 + 0	=	29
						2 + 9 = **11**
						1 + 1 = **2** ROOT LIFE PURPOSE

CASE STUDY 4: Martin Luther King, Jr.

Martin Luther King, Jr., was born on January 15, 1929.

JANUARY		15		1929		COMPOUND LIFE PURPOSE NUMBER
1	+	1 + 5	+	1 + 9 + 2 + 9	=	28
						2 + 8 = **10**
						1 + 0 = **1** ROOT LIFE PURPOSE

To view the complete, in-depth definitions for all 31 Day of Birth Numbers and all 48 Life Purpose Numbers, please refer to Chapter 3 (single digit numbers 1–9), Chapter 4 (double digit "master numbers" 11, 22, 33, 44) and Chapter 5 (double digit "compound" numbers 10–48).

CHAPTER 2

YOUR BIRTH NAME CODE

YOUR DESTINY NUMBER IS DERIVED FROM THE NAME ON YOUR BIRTH CERTIFICATE. It describes the nature of your work environment, specifically how you naturally use your gifts and activate your divine mission. Thus your Destiny Number is aligned with your career.

You are designed to express your Day of Birth Number and Life Purpose Number in a certain way. This "way" is your career environment, described by your Destiny Number.

For example, if your Day or Life Purpose Number resonates to the root number 3, then you must share joy and uplift others in some capacity. The key to HOW to turn this natural way of being into a thriving career is described by your Destiny Number. If your Destiny Number resonates to the root number 7, then your best career environment for expressing joy and uplifting others happens when you are working alone, in private, with plenty of time to think, read and listen. Ideally you have easy access to nature, since 7 is the number of serenity, contemplation, analysis, and inspiration. Your breakthroughs come in moments of silence. Your natural optimism and desire for self expression (3 Life Purpose or Day of Birth) are unlocked when you are in your own private quiet space, where timelessness exists and your mind can enter a kind of cathartics state of being...

On the other hand, if you have a **3** Day of Birth or Life Purpose and a Destiny Number that reduces to **8**, then you are meant to step up as a leader who inspires and motivates others from a joyful place, or you embody the connection between happiness and financial abundance, or you elevate others to lead from a internal place of joyful self expression, often through entrepreneurship.

Do this exercise with both your Day of Birth Number and Life Purpose Number—merge each of them with your Destiny Number to discover how you to best express your gifts, personality and strengths in a career environment.

Let's begin by calculating your birth certificate name first. It's best to learn how to add all the letters in your name before using an online calculator, so you can write down and feel your numbers in action!

How to Calculate Your DESTINY Number

Every person and entity has a name. The "Birth Name" is the third of the Three Important Numbers in your Birth Code. To calculate it, use the name on your birth certificate.

If you were adopted, please use the birth certificate name that was in place before you turned 6 months old. So, if the new adopted name was made official before you were 6 months of age, use that name. If it was changed after you turned 6 months old, use the original birth certificate name. You can still look at the new adopted name as a secondary influence.

Each letter resonates to a specific number. When calculating which number is aligned with which letter, we use the Pythagorean (Western) Numerology Alphabet system. It is a straight-forward system where letter A corresponds to the number 1, B to number 2, C to number 3 all the way to I to number 9, and then begins at letter J for number 1, and so on.

Use the following table to convert every individual letter in each of the names that make up your full birth certificate name into a number:

PYTHAGOREAN SYSTEM

1	2	3	4	5	6	7	8	9
A	B	C	D	E	F	G	H	I
J	K	L	M	N	O	P	Q	R
S	T	U	V	W	X	Y	Z	

Add up your birth certificate name to discover your Destiny Number:

1. Write the birth name down on a piece of paper (or type the birth name on your computer).

2. Assign each letter to the corresponding number in the alphabet, using the Pythagorean System above.

3. Count all the numbers for one total.

Your total Destiny Number then must be reduced to a single digit root number. As you discovered in Chapter 1, sometimes you need to reduce more than once to arrive at that single digit.

Important Tips on Suffixes in birth names:

1. Do not count the letters in "Jr" or "Sr." For example, "John Smith, Jr." is written as "JOHN SMITH" without "Jr."

2. Do not count I, II, or III. For example "John Smith, III" is calculated as "JOHN SMITH."

3. Count any foreign letters as if they did not have symbols—so å is a, ü is u, Æ is AE, œ is oe, and so on.

Let's look at the same celebrity case studies from Chapter 1 to learn how to calculate any Destiny Number from all the letters in a person's birth certificate name.

CASE STUDY 1:

Justin Timberlake's Birth Certificate Name is "Justin Randall Timberlake."

J	U	S	T	I	N		R	A	N	D	A	L	L
1	3	1	2	9	5		9	1	5	4	1	3	3

T	I	M	B	E	R	L	A	K	E	DESTINY NUMBER		
2	9	4	2	5	9	3	1	2	5	89		
										8 + 9 = 17		
										1 + 7 = 8 ROOT DESTINY		

Justin Timberlake's Destiny Number is **98/17/8**.
So, Justin Timberlake's Three Important Birth Numbers are:

Birthday: **1.31.1981**
1. Day of Birth: **31/4**
2. Life Purpose Number: **24/6**
3. Destiny Number **98/17/8**

First look up the meanings for single digit **Day of Birth** and **Life Purpose** Numbers **4** and **6** in Chapter 3. Given those meanings you'll notice that Justin is naturally methodical (4) and magnetic (6), disciplined, productive, grounded (4) and creative, responsible, compassionate (6) as well as not being afraid of work and making his own rules (4) and craving harmony and being fond of luxury (6).

How does he express these gifts in a career environment? Through his **Destiny Number 8**—look up the meaning for number 8 in Chapter 3. He is a natural leader, a strong, determined visionary, efficient and ambitious, patient, courageous, abundant and influential.

Now let's *combine* the meaning of Justin Timberlake's 4 Day of Birth and 6 Life Purpose numbers with his 8 **Destiny Number** to see the best career environment for him:

When Justin Timberlake is in a positive vibrational state, the career environment that allows him to express his natural gifts with greatest ease and joy is defined by Justin stepping up as an artistic, compassionate LEADER, a magnetic, creative VISIONARY, and a disciplined, hard-working INFLUENCER who uses his power and abundance in a positive, unique, and nurturing way, thereby being a source of courage to others.

Justin Timberlake's career as a singer-songwriter, actor and record producer ultimately defines his purpose and destiny.

CASE STUDY 2:

Mariel Hemingway's Birth Certificate Name is "Mariel Hadley Hemingway."

M	A	R	I	E	L		H	A	D	L	E	Y
4	1	9	9	5	3		8	1	4	3	5	7

H	E	M	I	N	G	W	A	Y	DESTINY NUMBER
8	5	4	9	5	7	5	1	7	110

$$1 + 1 + 0 = 2 \text{ ROOT DESTINY}$$

Now let's discover Mariel Hemingway's Three Important Birth Numbers:

Mariel Hemingway's Birthday: **11. 22.1961**
1. Day of Birth: **22/4**
2. Life Purpose Number: **23/5**
3. Destiny Number **110/2**

First look up the meanings for single digit **Day of Birth** and **Life Purpose** Numbers **4** and **5** in Chapter 1. Given those meanings you'll notice that Mariel is naturally disciplined and grounded (4) and adventurous and fearless (5), methodical, dependable and unique (4) and versatile, charming and resilient (5) as well as not being afraid of work and making her own rules (4) while craving freedom, movement, and choices (5).

How does she express these gifts in a career environment? Through her **Destiny Number 2**—look up the meaning for number 2 in Chapter 1. Mariel is highly sensitive, a peacemaker, with an active, imagination, is attuned to others, cooperative, patient, quiet, intuitive, and has an eye for detail.

Now let's *combine* the meaning of Mariel Hemingway's 4 Day of Birth and 5 Life Purpose numbers with her 2 **Destiny Number** to see the best career environment for her:

When Mariel Hemingway is in a positive vibrational state, the career environment that allows her to express her natural gifts with greatest ease and joy is defined by Mariel bringing energy into balance as a caring PEACEMAKER who is dependable as well as flexible, a PROPHET of freedom, a trusting CONFIDANTE, and a disciplined, hard-working diplomat who uses her adventurous spirit in a fun, unique, and kind way, thereby being a source of calmness and inspiration to others.

Mariel Hemingway's acting career coupled with her passion for living a balanced life—as a producer of videos on yoga and holistic living—ultimately defines her dedication to express her purpose and destiny for her highest good.

CASE STUDY 3:

Tony Robbins' Birth Certificate Name is "Anthony J. Mahavoric."

A	N	T	H	O	N	Y		J	
1	5	2	8	6	5	7		1	

M	A	H	A	V	O	R	I	C	DESTINY NUMBER
4	1	8	1	4	6	9	9	3	80
									8 + 0 = 8 ROOT DESTINY

Now let's discover Tony Robbins's Three Important Birth Numbers:

Birthday: **2.29.1960**
1. Day of Birth: **29/11/2**
2. Life Purpose Number: **29/11/2**
3. Destiny Number **80/8**

Look up the meanings for single digit **Day of Birth** and **Life Purpose** Numbers which are both **11/2** in Chapters 3 and 4, respectively. You'll notice that Tony Robbins has an "intensification" of the number 11/2. Given the meaning of 11/2, this intensification doubles up the impact and meaning of that master number in Tony's life: He is an inspirational teacher, able to balance the material and spiritual, a unique leader, highly creative, has a gift of connecting 1 on 1, and is a master of the present moment by channeling instantaneous creative solutions.

How does Tony Robbins express these gifts in a career environment? Through his **Destiny Number 8**—look up the meaning for number 8 in Chapter 1. He is a natural leader, a strong, determined visionary, efficient and ambitious, patient, courageous, abundant and influential.

Now let's *combine* the meaning of Tony Robbins' 11/2 Day of Birth and 11/2 Life Purpose numbers with his 8 **Destiny Number** to see the best career environment for him:

When Tony Robbins is in a positive vibrational state, the career environment that allows him to express his natural gifts with greatest ease and joy is defined by Tony defining his whole life as an inspirational LEADER, a dynamic TEACHER and VISIONARY, a practical and spiritual CHANNEL who uses his enthusiasm, power, and abundance in a unique and highly inspiring way, igniting an inner Fire in his followers.

Tony is an incredible teacher, coach, and leader. He has totally stepped into his purpose and destiny thereby creating a legacy that is for his and many others' highest good.

CASE STUDY 4:

Martin Luther King, Jr.'s, Birth Certificate Name was
"Michael King, Jr."

M	I	C	H	A	E	L		K	I	N	G
4	9	3	8	1	5	3		2	9	5	7

DESTINY NUMBER = 56

$5 + 6 = 11$

$1 + 1 = 2$ ROOT DESTINY

Martin Luther King, Jr.'s, Destiny Number is **56/11/2.**

Now let's discover Martin Luther King, Jr.'s, Three
Important Birth Numbers:

Martin Luther King, Jr.'s, Birthday: **1.15.1929**
4. Day of Birth: **15/6**
5. Life Purpose Number: **28/10/1**
6. Destiny Number **56/11/2**

Martin Luther King, Jr.'s, 56 Destiny reduces to the
"Master Number" 11 and a single digit 2.

First look up the meanings for King's single digit **Day of Birth** of 6 and **Life Purpose** Number **1** in Chapter 1. Given those meanings you'll notice that Martin Luther King, Jr. was a natural, authentic leader (1), deeply compassionate and needing to be of service (6), an accomplished and original thinker (1), responsible and loving to family and friends (6), determined and private (1) while having a magical, magnetic presence and craving harmony and beautiful surroundings (6).

How did he express these gifts in a career environment? Through his **Destiny Number 11/2**—look up the meanings for number 11 in Chapters 4 and 2 in Chapters 1 or 3. Martin Luther King, Jr., was an inspirational leader, a natural teacher, intuitive and a seeker of peace, spiritual, creative, attuned to energy, master of the present moment, a channel, gifted at connecting 1 on 1, imaginative, enthusiastic, and expressive.

Now let's *combine* the meaning of Martin Luther King, Jr.'s, 6 Day of Birth and 1 Life Purpose numbers with his 11/2 **Destiny Number** to see the best career environment for him:

When Martin Luther King, Jr., was in a positive vibrational state, the career environment that allowed him to express his natural gifts with greatest ease and joy is defined by King bringing disharmonious energy into balance as a loving PEACEMAKER, a PROPHET of Peace, an INSPIRATIONAL LEADER, and a SPIRITUAL TEACHER.

As an American Baptist minister and activist who became the foremost spiritual leader of the Civil Rights movement using peace and non violence (inspired by Ghandi), Dr. King was an inspirational teacher, peace-maker and dynamic leader who created dynamic, soul-level change in the spirit of love—for his and many others' highest good.

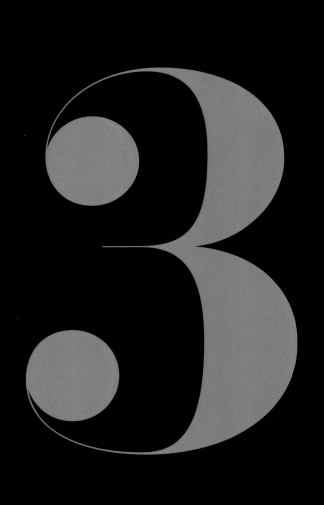

CHAPTER 3

SINGLE DIGITS 1–9 AND THE THREE TRIADS

NOW IT'S TIME TO DELVE INTO THE POSITIVE GIFTS AND SHADOW SIDE FOR ALL NINE SINGLE DIGIT ROOT NUMBERS. If one of your three numbers appears twice (for example, you have a 7 Day of Birth and a 124 Destiny which reduces to 7) then you have an "Intensification."

We begin with the Three Numerology Triads, since they reveal how each single digit belongs to a unique number "family."

The 1-5-7 "Mind" Triad

The three numbers that comprise the "Mind" triad are 1, 5, and 7. Those who have one or more of these three Mind numbers are analytical, intellectual, intuitive, ambitious, independent, witty, and psychic. This Mind triad is comfortable with information, both analyzing and gathering facts and figures, and using the mind to solve problems and make decisions. They enjoy learning and exploring new territory.

Mind triad people may have a tendency to worry or overanalyze—getting caught up in the net of information overload. Encouraging a Mind person to *feel* the outcome of their solutions in advance instead of *thinking* through them, may make them feel a tad uncomfortable—but is truly the way into experiencing that missing link—the blissful factor. Fortunately, Mind people have a natural intuitive side that is always ready to listen once they switch off (or at least turn down) their "inner analyst!"

The 2-4-8 "Manifestation" Triad

The three numbers that comprise the "Manifestation" triad are 2, 4, and 6. Those who have one or more of these three Manifestation numbers are by nature more patient, have a peaceful, grounding energy, use order and discipline to manifest results into physical reality, and are a stable influence. Manifestation triad people know how to get things done and overcome obstacles to do so. Thus, having a 2, 4, or 8 in your Three Important Birth Numbers, is an invitation to implement result after result, building a solid foundation for now and the future.

Manifestation people may have a tendency to implement before intuiting or feeling out the efficacy of their plans. So they may be perplexed when they don't achieve their intended result. This happens because their intentions were not fully aligned with how they feel before they go into manifestation mode. Taking the "heart" and "fun" out of the intention process, can lead to frustration. With their natural thirst to manifest, they just need to carve out some quality time to *enjoy* the process, introduce a sense of *play* and check into their feelings. Then, the outcomes of their steady implementation process will be extraordinary and lasting.

The 3-6-9 "Creation" Triad

Numbers 3, 6, and 9 form the Triad of Creation. Those people who have one or more of these three Creation numbers are by nature compassionate, loving, emotionally engaged, highly creative, nurturing, enthusiastic, social, and have a great need to be of service in order to uplift others. Creation triad people must have their heart engaged in every part of their life experience. Feeling good and expressing their good vibes in some way is their key to happiness. Thus they must have an outlet to talk, write, dance—create in any format of their choosing.

When expressing the shadow side of this triad, the person can get moody, dissipate energy through distractions, stop manifesting altogether and abdicate responsibilities. They can feel sorry for themselves and blame the world for what they perceive as unfair treatment. The best "cure" for distractions and doldrums is—go play and create. Laughter and humor are wonderful healing balms for the 3-6-9 triad to create a "pattern interrupt" and press the mood reset button! Their feelings are their soul-food, and so getting into a positive state allows them to feel valued, appreciated and loved again. Then they can share the love, uplift others and thrive. After all, to LOVE is their ultimate motivation.

A special note about this triad. The 3-6-9 triad governs the creation process. Thus, the building blocks of the universe reduce down to these three numbers. In astrology, for example, all the different "aspects" (connections between planets or angles) add up to numbers which reduce to either 3, 6, or 9, such as the 120° "Trine" which adds up to 3, the 90° "Square" which adds up to 9, and the 60° Sextile which adds up to 6 (Any aspect will reduce to 3, 6 or 9). The 24 hours in a day add up to 6, and 12 hours add up to 3. 60 minutes is 6.

Multiples of 3, 6, and 9 are repeated over and over again no matter which number is multiplied.

Use the three triads—Mind, Manifestation and Creation—to get a quick read on anyone. For example, if you know a person with a 10/**1** Day of Birth (which is in the MIND triad) and a 33/**6** Life Purpose (which is in the CREATION Triad) you can deduct that this person likes to analyze, think things through, craves independence, and is motivated (Mind) and also has a great capacity for compassion, enjoys helping and advising others, has good people skills, and must express their feelings (Creation).

These three Numerology Triads alone are a great starting point to gain instant understanding of a person's outlook and natural ways.

Number "0"

The Number 0 represents a unique power. It takes you to your Origins—Original Source. Where there is and always will be Only light, total Omnipotence. Even the word "Zero" ends with the letter O, representing 0. The full circle in O is both everything and nothing, full and empty. It is both a container and an entry into another dimension. It can hold all energy, while allowing all energy to pass through it. There is no time, just eternity.

Look at zero as the ultimate existential experience. Zero puts a divine sparkle into everything it touches. Zero holds divine light.

Meaning of Single Digit "Root" Numbers

Let's go now on a wonderful, life-changing journey and discover the secret drivers, divine gifts and direction for all nine single-digit numbers from 1 through 9.

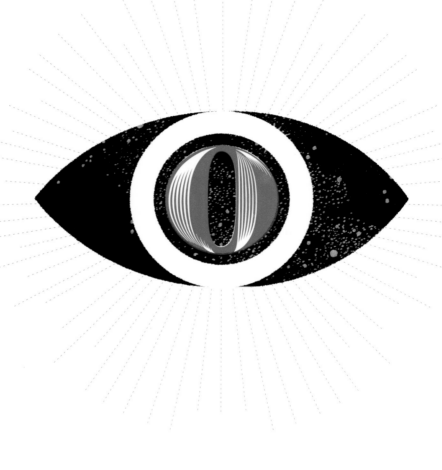

Use the following descriptions for your Day of Birth Number, Life Purpose Number, and Destiny Number.

Make a note of intensifications—when the same number repeats.

Pay attention to which numerology triad your Three Important Birth Code numbers belong to:

Are they **all grouped into one triad family?**

For example, all three of your Important Birth Code Numbers are either 2, 4, OR 8 thus representing the Manifestion Triad exclusively.

Or do they represent **two** of three triads?

For example your birth code is comprised of a 3 and a 9 (Creation) and a 5 (Mind).

Or do your three Important Birth Code Numbers **all belong to a different triad**?

Thus your birth code represents every triad, for example a 3 Day of Birth (Creation Triad), a 2 Life Purpose (Manifestation Triad), and a 7 Destiny (Mind Triad).

ROOT NUMBER 1

1 is the number of new beginnings and originality. It is the vibration of free will, individual pursuit, innovation, and daring. 1 represents courage and enthusiasm. 1 people follow their primary impulse. They are confident leaders who want to leave a legacy. A 1 person animates energy, always creating something new, and guides others to breakthroughs.

1's mind is always on fire. Putting the ideas into practice takes its form in unique ways. 1 seeks to stand out in some way and direct others. They usually become important and influential in some area of life.

Mediocrity frustrates 1s—they need to feel value and the original, intelligent spark of creation in everything and everyone. 1 represents the masculine aspect of our human experience.

1 is proud, dignified, and achievement oriented, and has a strong self-worth. 1 demands respect and feels set apart from others. 1 has strong views and definite beliefs, and protects those that are vulnerable. They are private and value their solitude.

1s are affectionate with those whom they love and trust. 1 is comfortable around younger people and children, though may at times feel a sadness arise from childhood memories. 1 tends to have impeccable taste with a penchant for the finer things in life.

Since 1s are naturally self-centric, and here to learn to be self-sufficient and self-reliant, they desire to be in love and be loved by a partner. This paradox exists perhaps because they need to explore being independent and then learn to be *inter-dependent*.

1 people have mental resources and an active imagination. Appealing to a 1's intelligence leads to the best results. 1s do not do well with authority, as they will eventually rebel and even turn aggressive. They need to

guard against over-analyzing and worrying about a future that is hypothetical. Staying focused on the present in a flowing, creative state of being allows 1 people to thrive and reach their highest goals, often with astounding speed.

Challenging expressions of 1:

1 people are good at starting but have a difficult time completing projects. Their pride can get the best of them. 1 does not respond well to criticism. 1 in its shadow expression is stubborn and will complain when ambitions are thwarted. 1 will only help others if they do exactly as the 1 expects of them. 1s get angry when ignored.

A 1 person can be boastful, aggressive, cynical, and egotistical, and even can turn to bullying others. Other out-of-alignment expressions are being indecisive, lacking initiative, being lazy, low confidence, or being easily swayed by others.

If you have hurt a 1 person in some way, share your apologies with humility and they will be accepted with grace.

1 people can attract resentment for their airs of superiority. They can be obstinate and do not accept opposition. Or they can be inconsiderate of other people's feelings even though they themselves are sensitive.

The way to harmony and peace is to be carefree and spontaneous, loosen the reigns of control, use their good humor, and tap into their love of discoveries, as this positive mindset aligns 1s to their heart center.

How to navigate the shadow tendencies of the number 1:

Affirmation: *I am at ONE with my mind, heart, and soul. I magically create opportunities to accomplish anything!*

ROOT NUMBER 2

2 is the number of peace, balance, and unity. 2 merges realities, bringing opposites together. They are the peacemakers; their patience and listening abilities are highly prized.

2 carries ancient wisdom, a sense of mysticism, and secrets, and has wonderful artistic gifts. It represents duality, pairs, couples, the feminine vibration, receptivity, and one-on-one engagement. 2 people are sensitive, so be gentle with them. 2 is connected to imagination and dreams.

2 people get along with pretty much anyone. They don't seek to measure up against others or impose their beliefs on them. They are peaceful people to be around, and they exude a calmness when making decisions.

2s have a need to look for advice, support, and approval from others. Their cautious approach requires a need to understand and know as much as they can before making a decision, and then proceeding with care. This gives 2s the gift of good judgment.

2s are excellent managers, as they have a touch of persuasion that opens doors for everyone to see eye-to-eye—often discreetly getting others to view things their way. This enables the 2 person to make major inroads in securing consensus between different parties, allowing them to open doors and succeed where others could not.

2 is the first vibration in the 2-4-8 Manifestation triad. Thus 2s are naturally responsible, conscientious, and efficient. 2s are usually humble, but can initially lack self-confidence.

2 people are psychic, though they may keep that side of themselves secret. They are sensitive to other people's feelings, sensing them instantly. Their highly developed intuition serves them well when they meet people, since their natural shyness can lead them to not trust others easily. 2s are generous friends and make great companions. They're interested in the psychology of human nature due to their acute observation skills and ability to intuit body language, sounds, and facial expressions. This makes them excellent observers.

2s are naturally romantic. One of their main lessons is to be in partnership with lovers, friends, and associates without losing their independence and sense of self. Not falling into co-dependent relationship patterns is a major lesson for any 2 person. 2s are affectionate and tender. They have a primal urge to please others.

Due to their sensitive nature, 2 people are secretive. But they are wonderful conversationalists and can naturally get others to reveal parts of themselves. When they approach their goals, they are the opposite of 1 people who just go for it—2s will move forward, then course-correct. This zig-zag pattern towards their goals gives them a sense of balance. A 2 person will usually attract financial well-being—if anything, it is rare to see them struggling in conditions of poverty. However, if trained to have a "poverty-conscious" mindset, 2s must consciously extricate themselves from this paradigm first before experiencing their natural gift to attract prosperity. 2s are giving with their resources. They find it more difficult to accept gifts, feeling inadequate if they accept support, especially financial.

2s trust others implicitly. They can't imagine anyone having a "bad" intention or being anything but kind and noble. This means they believe what others tell them. So they must learn to discern between what feels right and what feels just a little "off"—use their intuitive gifts to separate the manipulators from those who will not take advantage of their kind hearts and good faith.

A 2 person loves to dream and live in their imaginary, idealistic world. These sensitive, kind souls are highly adaptable and intuitive, giving them the qualities they need to fulfill their beautiful dream of bringing peace, love and harmony to the world. In their most positive state, 2s are a true blessing to everyone around them.

How to navigate and heal the shadow tendencies of the number 2:

Bypass any division or indecision through listening, deep breathing and gratitude.

Challenging expressions:

A 2 person may have a tendency to fear the unknown and be unusually cautious. They need highly sensitive support to come to terms with the unfamiliar. In fact, 2s can fear every kind of pain or loss, allowing their active imagination to fuel their fears and worries. They may appear calm and balanced, but this can also hide a neurotic, touchy, nervous disposition. If they feel hurt by someone, they will retreat into silence and even shut down.

Due to their natural humility, 2s, when out of alignment, can sometimes slip into feeling inadequate and suffer from low self-esteem. This sets up a situation where they can easily get depressed and will create problems for themselves to almost "prove" their perceived state of lack. The 2-4-8 Manifestation triad that number 2 belongs to is meticulous and demands thorough attention to detail—but the sensitive 2 person can go overboard and demand too much of themselves. Expectations that are set too high can spiral into complexes and inhibited behavior, as they doubt their own abilities and react fearfully when the unexpected shows up at their doorstep. This self-criticism is a big lesson for the 2 to overcome, so they stay centered and live their life free of inner conflict.

Being in a secure, loving home base is integral for their equilibrium across the spectrums in their life. Otherwise they will lose their sense of equilibrium. This is when 2s can become bitter and broken. Since conflict and a disharmonious environment have a detrimental effect on 2s, they must always have a "safe place" to go to feel loved and nurtured, otherwise they will lash out and be temperamental. Loud noise, aggressive violent movies, and blasting music will also harm the energetic field around a 2 person, and can easily throw them off balance.

2s will sacrifice much to get their life back into harmony. It is important for them to accept that life is filled with **both** positive and negative situations, so that they don't react to the challenging moments with tension, depression, and inner turmoil.

Their shyness may make them "freeze" around strangers, but once they feel their heart engaged in a conversation, they open it to others. They are deeply affected by rude behavior.

2s can be cautious and may not easily take a chance. They also can become possessive of things and people. Indecision can lead to feeling separate and divided.

2s must release their desire to please and be "perfect;" otherwise doubt and indecision will run their lives in circles. Their need to please can lead them to sacrifice their own unique ideas for someone else's cause—thus 2s need to maintain boundaries.

They must not get preoccupied with unimportant matters that create a false sense of connection *without yielding meaningful results*; the wasted time reinforces a sense of inadequacy and incompletion. 2s must always discern between what matters and what does not—what is for their highest good, and what is not.

Relaxation is the key for a 2 to maintain inner harmony and peace. In this place of serenity their moods and emotions won't get repressed or overwhelm them. Daily deep breathing, exercise, and meditation are wonderful and necessary for 2s. Bypass division, separation, or indecision through listening, deep breathing, and gratitude.

Affirmation: *I am indivisible. I breathe deeply and feel connected to the Divine at all times. I am grateful for every experience that comes my way and see hidden benefits to each encounter in my life.*

ROOT NUMBER 3

A 3 person is creative, action-oriented, truthful, and radiates with joy. They are fluid in how they move through their life experiences and love to explore everything from their heart-center. 3 is connected to Truth, Fertility, and Creation. It is the number representing the Trinity of Mother-Father-Child, which governs creation. 3 people are usually talented, vivacious, interested in many things, and brilliant. They love to learn.

3 is fiercely independent, seeking total freedom of movement. 3s must express themselves in some capacity; they must communicate. They always have something to say! They are fierce advocates of freedom of speech and expression. Their natural yearning for renewal and birth gives them tremendous powers of creation.

3 is infused with compassion, tenderness, and a loving, affectionate disposition. They are magnetic. 3s are impressionable, especially if others appeal to their generous nature or show them appreciation. 3 people have a great sense of humor and a cheerful disposition. Their optimism is contagious. They are the most positive, uplifting people to be around.

3s can take any challenging situation and move quickly through bitterness into a place of acceptance. Their ability to "see" future positive outcomes stems from an uncanny "birds-eye" view that allows them to fully move through trauma and come out the other side. These talents, coupled with their natural gifts of expression and outgoing personalities, make 3s adept at helping anyone feel good. They are experts at comfortably mixing with any group and have a knack for adjusting quickly to different personalities or changing situations.

3s are born to inspire. They cast a spell by just being delightful, motivating others to act through their passionate enthusiasm, happiness, positive mindset, and optimistic attitude. Their spontaneity blends with an effortless capacity to connect with anyone. Their charm coupled with their magnetism relaxes anyone with whom they make contact.

For 3s, everything comes down to furthering a deep ideal, something they are so passionate about that they can't imagine anyone else not sharing the same ideal with them. This ideal is their truth. They will leave no stone unturned to find the truth. Thus they make great detectives. 3s can spot a lie in a second.

3s appreciate success due to the pleasures that achievement brings. They like to spoil themselves and their loved ones (and need to watch their wallets).

3s thrive when they can travel; being with others, seeing the world, and going on journeys wakes up their innate creativity and yearning for independence. Plus they love to explore other countries, cultures, music, and people. 3s are also deeply spiritual.

3s love defending the underdog and are advocates for animals. They will take risks; when they couple their natural passion with their willingness to take a chance, their impact is beautiful. Their delightful, charming, magnetic personalities are a breath of fresh air invoking a lightness of being.

Having a higher education makes 3s feel part of the higher ideals and philosophies they so cherish. They must have a total sense of independence in any marriage.

A balanced 3 will not succumb to moodiness or de-pression and will easily forgive themselves as easily as forgiving others. Having a good circle of friends can help 3s to express their ideas and feelings, though the key to their happiness is to engage in creative activities.

The key to a happy, meaningful life is for a 3 to *focus and specialize.*

3 people must persevere in their chosen specialty and not get distracted by frivolous activities. They must only promise what they can deliver and intend to accomplish.

When 3s know they are uplifting people, nothing will stop them. In their natural, connected state, 3 people are luminous, vibrant beings of joy.

Challenging expressions:

3s can and will multitask; however their tendency to scatter results in wasted energies when they are tired or out of alignment. They can delay or dilute the impact of their divine mission if they don't learn to how to focus and specialize in one direction at a time. Vacillation can lead to indecision or going on tangents for hours, days or weeks at a time. 3s like to begin projects, but may have a more difficult time completing them.

A 3 gets bored if not engaged, and may slack off if they lack self-motivation. 3s need to play and have fun, but can go too far and forget about their responsibilities. This happens especially when they don't have the organization to help them stay focused. Thus, they can get lazy about practicing and developing their gifts. 3s believe anything is permitted because it is so easy for them to attain success, so they use their congenial nature as an "escape" to chill more than necessary.

When 3s stop consistently pursuing goals, they may attribute their lack of practice to *other* factors. But in the end, most inaction and lack of commitment is due to their lazy attitude. This confusion about the **origin** of their lack of initiative can throw them for a loop. It occurs especially when 3s encounter mental blocks or tiredness and won't work through their resistance with a conscious decision to ACT.

3s can be wise and philosophical, then witty and funny the next moment, while abdicating discipline. This results in a lack of steady growth. A 3 person also may have the tendency to be talkative, sometimes compulsively.

There can always be too much of a good thing, and 3s can exaggerate and even be superficial and "fake" or may make promises they can't keep.

The quickest cure for a negative emotional state or depression is to BE CREATIVE. Express yourself in whichever way you want to. Then you reconnect with the beauty and joy in your soul and are happily on track and back in the flow again.

Affirmation: *I am happily engaged with what I love to do. I lavish my focus and full attention on activities that uplift me. I spend time with those who allow me to feel light and free.*

ROOT NUMBER 4

4 is a grounding frequency with a mysterious quality. 4s are practical, trustworthy, and hands-on. When you commit to something, you complete it. You're sought after for your reliability, organizational skills, calm demeanor, self-discipline, attention to detail, and responsibility. But 4 is also an **enigma.**

4 always has one foot in the future; this is the inventor wanting to go the unconventional route. Your ideas and values are ahead of their time, unconventional, and even prophetic. 4 favors individualism, originality, and sudden, unexpected events. As a living paradox (organized AND unpredictable) you are seldom fully understood, but it is what makes you so unique.

There is a "genius" quality to your 4 vibration that allows your natural curiosity to go off the beaten path. You have the focus and discipline to explore your hunches.

Though you are eager to explore all possibilities, you resist changing personal habits. This four-square "box" can be your hiding place to avoid taking responsibility for your own growth.

The lesson for a 4 person is to stay connected to Earth while exploring the wonderful gifts of creation. Then the discoveries and shifts are *mirrored* in their personal lives as well, as reluctance to make personal changes dissipates.

The balance between heaven and earth is reflected in the merging of intuition and intelligence—applied equally across all four areas of human life—physical, mental, emotional, and spiritual.

Thus 4 symbolizes the REAL reason for our life on Earth: *We are divine beings of Light having a human experience*.

Living in a clean, organized environment is important for you to stay balanced and healthy. Be sure to "feng-shui" your home and workplace often.

You love being part of a family and cherish your friends. You are tolerant and compassionate. Money and status are not of great interest to you. You mix with all people, not caring about rank or class. It's the "inner genius" in you—your surroundings might go unnoticed in favor of your imagination! You live for this moment.

Challenging expressions:

When you are energetically out of alignment, a rigid approach to life will appear. Being headstrong can also lead to arguments. A tendency to work long hours may turn into over-work, so be careful about crossing the line when it comes to fulfilling tasks. If you notice it gets to the point where you get too busy, make time to simply enjoy life. Emotionally you can close down.

You may get too serious at times, forgetting to go with the flow. When you find yourself not responding to humor, loosen up! Hanging on to old habits or living in a disorganized space will exasperate being stuck.

Guard against being careless and not fulfilling your responsibilities. A real disconnection from the positive expression of your number 4 results in dishonesty and a completely undisciplined lifestyle. You can inflict needless pain on yourself through envy, self-pity, and resentment of others. You will waste time and other resources while fixating on comparing yourself to others or feeling guilt, rather than lifting yourself out of the situation by taking a step of faith, owning your experience of it, and being accountable. DOING something valuable sets you back on track!

Affirmation: *I am whole, I am complete, I am more than enough, I am who I am—I live and let live.*

ROOT NUMBER 5

5 expands your original creative ideas through a keen intellect. You are adept at capturing all the various angles of a question with perception. You are connected to higher consciousness by your keen sense of freedom and adventure.

Exploring the unknown is your forte, physically or in your mind. You want to taste, see, smell, touch, and hear as much as you can. Though this can result in distractions, you are designed to handle multiple tasks at one time, depending on the nature each task requires your full attention or not. The 5 vibration is by nature sensual and spiritual.

You have a charm that makes you attractive. When you feel fulfilled and happy, your enthusiasm makes you irresistible, and you become the center of attention in any gathering.

Connection is one of your key themes; you use media to meet others, gather information, and share your message, all with the goal of bringing people together. 5 governs groups or crowds of people, making you an adept social networker, performer, writer, or speaker. You enjoy big crowds! This gift of connection also makes you a wonderful salesperson. This persuasion power and your natural charm aligns you magically with anyone who experiences your words, music, art, or message.

The 5 vibration is alert and bright. You have an innate connection to your surroundings that makes you extremely fine-tuned, noticing everything in detail.

You are adaptable and thrive when there is movement; stagnation and boredom are your greatest fears. You are the intrepid adventurer, enjoying anything that opens your heart and mind to NEW things, ideas, and cultures. Being fearless is something you teach others just by who you are. Being so engaged in the moment makes you flexible and versatile. You win people over with your irresistible charm and wit, helping you create momentum to bring your divine gifts to a greater audience.

Freedom of movement is integral to your life. You may change where you live, travel, or wander all over the world looking for inspiration and excitement. You also can change your mind, sometimes abruptly from one moment to the next. Oscillation is the nature of the 5, also due to your restless, adventurous nature. You need to feel your imagination engaged. Stimulation of all your senses is an important factor in your well-being.

This excitement factor shows your ability to dazzle with your brilliance. Applause and accolades are natural by-products for you when you live at your highest vibrational frequency. Your personality is vivacious. Due to your alignment to subtle energetics, you have a great sensitivity for beautiful things, both artistic and intellectual. Just be aware that you tend to keep from emotionally engaging with ideas or people, and this can lead to an indifference about relationships.

As a 5 person, you are an agent of change for others. Your enthusiasm and daring exhibit a wonderful zest for life. It's as if you have the radiant mind of a child in your heart throughout your life. Your willingness to experience all that the world has to offer is both inspiring and motivational. Setbacks don't affect you for long; you are able to rebound quickly and move on living in the present moment.

Wherever you are, something is "happening." You love life, adventure, and liberty. You may fluctuate from feeling exalted to down for seemingly no reason except that others just don't understand how intensely you **experience** life. Your approach is one of total immersion.

Challenging expressions:

You may be critical when you are not energetically aligned with the positive expression of number 5, and this will lead to an urge to spot mistakes. Try not to be impatient when pointing them out.

You over-analyze people and situations. Logic appeals to you; however, you must open up the tenderness in your heart. Getting analytical at the expense of heart-to-heart connections, especially in your intimate relationships, can lead to endings. Using your instincts to navigate love, instead of intellectualizing the experience, is important if you are to maintain deep relationships.

You can be high-strung, have a nervous disposition, and crave change for the sake of change. Guard against impulsive actions and reactions. Any restlessness you have can be channeled into doing something new!

Addiction is another shadow side of this number. If you go too far, you forgot to use discernment. You may also enter and exit relationships quickly, rather than allowing them to evolve and grow.

If you find yourself criticizing others while not being responsible for your own life, you will vacillate through life blindly, not seeing a need to course-correct, not recognizing the valuable feedback coming your way, and not benefitting from the experiences that would enable you to mature emotionally.

Your attention is captured by many things at once, so you may not stay true to your *initial* impulses. Patience and learning how to center your magnificent gifts is the key for you to maintain calm and peace AND your delightful enthusiasm for life.

Affirmation: *I sing a song of delight. I take pleasure in everything I encounter. I surrender. I feel blessed!*

ROOT NUMBER 6

You are compassionate, loving, and responsible to your family and friends. You have a calming influence on others. 6 is aligned with beauty.

The key to the number 6 is nurturing others, being of loving service to others, being supportive and utterly devoted. You naturally want to share your advice. Inevitably people, friends, even strangers, will come to you and tell you their deepest secrets. You exude a warmth, compassion, and wisdom. Make sure you consciously create boundaries, otherwise you will feel energetically depleted. Also, make sure you make room in your life to nurture **yourself** to recharge your vibrational field. You love to give, and you must learn to receive the bounty of love life has to offer!

You love affection and hugs and are generous. And when you walk into a room, people take note!

6 governs human love and romance as well as money and abundance. Once you commit to a partnership you are devoted. This devotion extends to your loved ones and friends, who genuinely love you. You can get sentimental and idealistic. You are attuned to exhibiting good manners and are tasteful, yet will not shy away

from expressing yourself when you feel passionate about something.

To attract abundance, you must surround yourself with high aesthetics. Jarring noises, conflict, arguments, discord, jealousy, and unresolved issues are best eliminated or dealt with as quickly as possible for you to pursue the rest of your day at peace.

Your artistic side needs to be expressed. Surround yourself with beauty to feel good and whole. You love having your favorite colors and artwork in your home. Living in a place of serenity and beauty pleases you.

Money is attracted to you. Sometimes it can appear without much effort through inheritances or sponsors, but just as often it is your through your talents and abilities.

You are creative and must find an outlet to express your artistic gifts. The sound of your voice carries healing. And your smile is irresistible!

You are attuned to justice, seeking to find the underlying fair response to any situation. You are good at finishing projects once you get started.

When a 6 is not energetically aligned with their highest good:

6 out of alignment can lead to a controlling and interfering nature, where you meddle in other people's business. You'll argue your point to stay in power and cause a lot of disruption.

You can be a perfectionist, and this can lead to criticism of others. Sometimes you can resort to self-righteous behavior. Another shadow side of the 6 expression is total self-absorption.

Money matters can range from a spectrum from where you overspend and be too extravagant or go the other way and be extremely stingy. You need to watch your sweet tooth!

You may want to follow the path of least resistance (and keep a false sense of harmony). You can be careless concerning your responsibilities, especially fulfilling your divine mission. This will create a quality of being a "drifter," someone who does not make commitments to themselves and would rather "go with the flow." Your indecision, laziness, and feeling like you are being inconvenienced by choosing to commit to something, will make you the root cause of your failed half-hearted attempts. It also creates a spiraling tendency to magnify difficulties and obsess on problems.

To accomplish something meaningful and joyful, you must be *motivated internally and externally* to do anything—preferably through a goal or deadline—so as to overcome your occasional passive nature. Then you will shower the world with your loving radiance and brilliance!

Affirmation: *I share my love freely and generously. I practice using my gifts every day. I nurture myself. I care deeply about my divine mission to uplift others through love and joy.*

ROOT NUMBER 7

7 is the spiritual seeker, the mindful philosopher, and brilliant analyzer. You are driven to understand the mysteries of life. You are comfortable with secret subjects, the healing modalities, and usually have vivid dreams. You love to learn. Ultimately 7 is the number of spiritual completion.

7 can bridge anything, making connections between ideas and subjects that seemingly have no common ground, such as good and evil, light and dark. 7s can experience sudden profound shifts in their lives that take them by total surprise. The effect of the lightning bolt also makes 7 a "change agent." Often their presence alone can soothe and heal.

7 has a good memory and enjoys looking back at history to understand the present. A 7 person often has unorthodox, unique beliefs and values.

Due to their quest for knowledge, 7 people need to travel extensively at some point in their lifetime, or read many books about other cultures.

Financially it is important for 7s to have a nest-egg. Otherwise they get nervous about the future. This anxious tendency can interfere with their ultimate mission to be a channel for new wisdom.

As a 7 person, you look deeply at everything. You are an observer of the mysteries of life, a seeker of wisdom, and a natural researcher. You do best when you have extended periods of time alone.

Your views and values can at times be mysterious to others, as your quest for wisdom possibly changed the beliefs of your early life helped you connect your divine nature.

7 carries tremendous intelligence. You can be taken aback at times by the lack of understanding in others. You like to approach life from a logical perspective, yet eventually must merge intuition with logic to get to the deeper mysteries you yearn to solve. Specializing in any field suits you well, as you can delve into the infinite depths. If you ever feel the well has dried up, find another source of life to satisfy your curiosity. You're not a fan of anything frivolous or superficial.

You do not like to be under anyone's watchful eye! Any entity that invades your privacy is not welcome. When you enter a space, you feel what's going on, even though you'd never let on about it. This is what makes 7 a number of holding secrets.

If a 7 person goes into the creative arts, their ability to both learn and intuitively channel makes them magnetic performers, writers, or artists.

In your intimate relationships, you need privacy. You can be loving and devoted if you don't expect your partner to live up to your long list of ideals. Others need to earn their trust with you, but once they have it, you embrace them with complete non-judgment and openness.

You thrive when you are in nature, especially near the ocean. 7 rules rest, rejuvenation, meditation, and sabbaticals. Refresh your heart, mind, and soul with long stays in places that feel like spiritual sanctuaries.

The bridge that 7 symbolizes will be a metaphor for growth all your life. Bring the sacredness of bridging light and dark, seen and unseen, into your daily life. Make your life a ceremony, a devoted song to Spirit/Source/God. You understand the reason for darkness, and you, as the lightning bolt of truth, radiate brilliance. You are a beacon of light in the world. Shining your light in darkness is your divine gift. Opening up the sacred halls of wisdom within you will give you direct access to the truth, as revealed in the records of time and timelessness.

Always remember, your divine mission can benefit a big community of like-minded souls—and then reach out to inspire the world.

Challenging expressions:

Due to your wisdom and natural quest for knowledge, you can get impatient with those who in your mind cannot "catch on" fast enough. Also, your perfectionism may turn you into a critic with a need for perfect results rather than being open to what is for the highest good of the situation. Guard against being cynical about life.

Balance your strong energy with time for playfulness. Otherwise you will focus on the powerful, accomplishment qualities of the 7 at the expense of joy and love.

You can be secretive, not revealing much about your true motivations. It's natural for you to keep your own issues private, yet not at the expense of being distrustful, or not trusting of others. In intimate relationships it is important for you to be vulnerable *emotionally,* not just *intellectually.*

When out of alignment you get pessimistic and frustrated. Know, this is when you try to direct your AHA moments in an obsessive way, rather than being a channel for Light and Love, without conditions on how or in what area that wisdom is to stream through you. A change of place or time in nature will usually help you reconnect quickly!

Affirmation: *I am Truth embodied. My Soul is my true home. I live to share the Light of Wisdom.*

ROOT NUMBER 8

8 is the vibration of leadership and strength, abundance, financial security, and power. 8 people have a vision that must be made practical. Thus 8 governs entrepreneurship and the executive. 8s are responsible and patient, allowing them to take an idea from its fruition to a successful outcome. It is natural for an 8 person to at some point in their life to experience obstacles, but they are designed to be overcome to gain confidence and strength. As an 8, you use challenges as stepping stones to success.

You are shy and reserved by nature. It is not immediately obvious that you have the fortitude to push forward, but you persist every step of the way, and eventually reach your goal.

8 represents making visions (messages from Spirit) real, bringing them to Earth and materializing them into goods that can be exchanged for money.

8 is aligned with business, in that this vibration takes a vision (spirit), creates a product or service (matter), puts it out into the world (enterprise) and in return receives payment for that product or service. This is one of the core spiritual and human energy exchanges to life. Both the spiritual and material realms represented by the number 8 are necessary to experience fulfillment and abundance. In some way or another an 8 person will be focused on money manifestation. Once their soul is completely free to manifest those messages from Spirit, 8 people realize their dreams of lasting abundance and fulfillment. Often, they end up as an example or teacher of spiritual, manifestation, and/or financial laws. An 8 person is meant to lead in some capacity.

8s are realistic and have great organizational skills. Your innate patience and intelligence allows you to excel at anything. You are born with a desire to take on responsibilities, so it is rare to find an 8 who is careless, since they pride themselves on living up to the highest expectations. Their reliability is legendary, and so is their warmth.

8s like to keep a strong image of themselves, but they do care about what others feel about them, especially when it comes to their accomplishments, and do (privately) enjoy compliments.

8s have an advanced sense of what is ethical and true, representing honor, impartiality, and dignity in everything they say and do. They also like to mix with dignitaries, seeking the company of important, influential people.

Share your resources with others in a philanthropic way. When positively aligned 8s can materialize anything. Their persistence, courage, and cooperative nature allow 8s to accomplish anything they set their mind to when it comes to working with others. 8 people are ambitious, enjoy challenges, and strive to be the best they can be. If they create something that fulfills them at soul-level, they will be successful. They can act as instruments of positive shifts in other people's lives.

As friends they are loyal, dedicated, and sweet with those they trust and care for deeply. However, due to their need to appear strong, 8s can feel lonely, with a great need to be loved and cherished. If a dear friend or family member needs them, the 8 person will make sacrifices for them. They will do the same for an ideal.

You as an 8 person are only attracted to quality and will not be seen shopping for second-hand clothes. You value the best. This is because you are aligned with the vibration of longevity.

Your dreams are never small! Everything you do has to exhibit your highest expectations of what is "the best." 8s have the inner courage, natural leadership, and vision to achieve greatness in any field. Their enjoyment of challenges and creating the best possible outcome for the highest good of all makes them unstoppable and wonderful contributors and influencers.

Challenging expressions:

An 8 out of alignment is egotistical, materialistic, and forceful—or succumbs to passive and powerless behavior. Their longing for success can outweigh their desire for happiness. Thus 8s must pay attention to their heart; if there is a feeling of loneliness or a sense of longing for something that is missing, an 8 must not be afraid to pursue happiness with the same wisdom, maturity, and discipline that they devote to their divine mission.

8s are demanding of themselves and transfer that quest for excellence and success onto others. You may take your ambitious drive too far. You will work without reservation for many hours to achieve your goal, but can forget to stop and smell the roses. Eventually this lack of appreciation along the way can lead to frustration and dissatisfaction.

Your dedication to the pursuit of your vision is commendable if you pay attention when you feel restless. If you don't, you might eventually react with anger when provoked, or exhibit a suctioning of strength in your physical body that translates into health conditions or a need for rest.

Guard against being egotistical and vindictive, obstinate, intolerant, and stubborn.

Affirmation: I give everything to inspire others to be the best they can be. My deeds are my expressions of wealth and well-being. I am enriched by helping to enrich others.

ROOT NUMBER 9

9 symbolizes evolution and an enhancement of psychic abilities. A 9 person is warm, outgoing, and loving with a dramatic flair, exuding a magnetic personality that allows him or her to get along with pretty much anyone. 9s are compassionate, romantic, kind, empathetic, patient, tolerant, and wise. You as a 9 are an inspirational and compassionate humanitarian with great idealism and strong willpower. Your imagination knows no bounds! And you absolutely love to give.

You have a powerful personality and you can use it to fulfill your greatest desire—to be useful to others by manifesting inspirational accomplishments and/or beneficial products or results. You represent *leadership by example*. You *live* your talk. You want your high ideals to inspire others, so they too experience their highest potential.

Your sweet-natured soul does not like seeing anyone in pain. When you see someone who is suffering, you reach out to them since you truly care about how others feel. You are a natural at teaching, healing, giving counsel through the highest values of love and beauty. Your goal is to raise the vibrational awareness of humanity.

You are here to help people, often through major transitions. To have the capacity to love deeply, without judgment or expectation, you yourself experienced hardship and tests. Those who are born to help others, experience the pain and loss themselves to forgive and have compassion at the deepest level of the human experience.

You understand people from all walks of life. You respect their various qualities and missions. You also love giving back. Your sensitive, artistic nature blends with your quest for perfection. As a leader, you demand only the best from yourself.

Your main lesson is to elevate what is seemingly ordinary into something extraordinary and meaningful.

You are honest and direct, penetrating directly to the heart of the matter. Other people's dishonesty, manipulation, or indirectness can catch you off-guard, so you need to learn to be more cautious with others, but not when you are teaching. Another quality to guard against is your impatience with those who think more slowly than you do.

No detail escapes your keen observation. You are conscious of all energy, subtle and visible, happening around you.

In relationships, you may strive to be in control. You may keep your distance, which results in a lack of true intimacy. You can be an enigma in this way, due to your warm, generous nature and your lack of commitment to a serious relationship.

You approach life with total passion and a profound intensity. Your vibrant and noble nature, enthusiasm, and generosity are noted by everyone in your presence.

Challenging expressions:

When you are energetically out of alignment you hold onto resentments or memories. You can shut down emotionally. Guard against being arrogant, tyrannical, or dishonest. An abdication of leadership can result in you closing your mind to wisdom and drifting through life aimlessly, dissipating your gifts. Frustration is a sign that you must reconnect with your heart-center and surrender to love.

Guard against focusing on limitations. This will push you to want to control others, since you are not healing your own sense of lack within first. Shift your focus onto creating beauty, love and excellence. Your role is to exude the joy of living a life to its highest potential. When you focus on what is for your highest good, your emotional touchiness will naturally disappear.

You can be stubborn, reacting with aggressive action and creating conflict as a result. Though your temper can rise to a boil quickly, you can just as quickly move on, ready to forgive and forget.

Your natural inclination to be direct can turn into a frankness that is too aggressive. Refrain from reacting instantaneously especially when the result is biting in nature.

Deep down you can have a fear of rejection. You need reassurance that you are appreciated, understood, respected, and loved.

Affirmation: *I serve others with love and wisdom. I stay true to my heart, leading always with love and for the highest good of all.*

CHAPTER 4

MASTER NUMBERS 11–99

NOW WE WILL ENTER THE REALM OF DOUBLE DIGIT NUMBERS 11, 22, 33, 44, 55, 66, 77, 88, AND 99, ALSO REFERRED TO AS "MASTER NUMBERS." Master Numbers are an intensification of a single digit number, so the core meaning of the single digit before it is doubled, is incorporated in a new experience, which takes on messages of the single and double digit and *blends* them into a *new* vision. Master Numbers by nature carry a greater responsibility than single digit vibrations.

Master Number 11

When 1 becomes 11, you embody the *original creative mind* and *leadership* number 1 and elevate it into 11 as the INTUITIVE MASTER, creating an experience of double new beginnings and Enlightened Leadership.

11 is supreme balance. Thus you as an 11 symbolize both the seen and unseen, which need to be brought into equilibrium. However, there is an illusion heaven and earth, visible and invisible, are separate, and you must bypass this illusion of division by uniting seemingly separate energies and goals. When you do, you will stop feeling a sense of incompletion and division running through your life.

As a "Master Number" you are being asked to master something at a high level. For the 11 you are mastering listening to your inner voice. Anytime you feel a sense of separation or division, tune in. This division could appear from a person or an interfering idea or ignorance. If you refuse to see BOTH sides, listen, and understand, you will prevent a rebalancing of energy to occur. In all cases of conflict or separation your role is to find out the source of opposing energy. Then the magical shift happens when you understand the Law of Opposites. That to experience Light you must also know Darkness. Then, exquisite harmony and peace infuse your heart as you listen intently.

Any nervousness, which comes because of 11 ruling light and electrical currents, can be healed through establishing routine and order in your life.

Your overall divine mission is to delve into the mysteries and miracles of Life. All becomes ONE within you. When you enter the Temple of Awareness, you have made a choice to live fully, with total acceptance of every situation that appears before you as being by your design, your beckoning—and always for your highest good. No matter how it appears!

Channeling a gift is the highest expression of this number. The gift is always bringing forth brand new information and inspiration—the initial experience of the unknown, thus making the unknown visible.

As an 11, you illuminate the truth. You have a choice to illuminate negative or positive energy, but you *will* channel energy and bring it to light. To prepare to channel what is *for your highest good,* it is important for you to discover your "inner teacher." Reconnecting to your inner voice is another way of describing your conscious engagement with your spiritual guides. You also receive great inspiration through symbols, music, art, and sacred geometry. Aligning to your soul opens up a universe of wisdom that you can access at will, instantaneously, and then share with others. It is keeping the balance that allows you to open up your creative vessel and let the divine pour through the 11.

You must always choose which endeavors in your life bring unity, and which cause separation. You will need to get off the fence and make a choice. That choice will enable you to enter the 11 gateway, take that risk and live fully in the present moment. This is when you feel whole. Once the way to unity is recognized, honored, and practiced continuously, you leave the struggle and division behind. You feel at peace. It is in the act of surrender that you fulfill your role to be a Master of Light and Love.

If you don't step through the gateway, explore your inner world—both the light and the darkness—you will project your fantasies and neuroses on others instead and eventually sabotage your goals. Life is filled with paradoxes, so there is no reason to doubt the importance of every experience as being valid. If you exclude exploring all sides of an issue you leave out part of the human experience. Your role is to be unconditional in your tolerance of those people and experiences that seem different. Then your 11 gateway is totally about freedom and unconditional love.

In exploring the dark and the light, the seen and the unseen, nothing escapes you and you walk the world an avatar of love. Instead of fighting injustice, you heal. Instead of resisting oppression and pain, you understand that ALL that happens to you has been called in by your soul. Nothing happens to us that is not ultimately for our highest good.

As an 11, you understand there is a veil of illusion—maya—that appears once we are born on Earth, protecting us from knowing everything we've experienced and will experience. Otherwise we would be overwhelmed. That veil is lifted for a bit every time we enter the 11 portal. In the entering of the gateway, light beams through our third eye and reveals our true divine origin. We become "seers" enlightened by entering the light. This is the moment to moment enlightenment, the union with love we so yearn for. So, the more you as an 11 trust and surrender to your intuition, the higher you raise your vibration.

Anyone who crosses your path will be enchanted by your undeniable charisma. You change people by the sheer influence of your powerful aura. For you personally this spiritual essence appears as unexpected windfalls, seemingly coincidental, that appear in synchronicity with your goals, guiding you to the light so that you can play the leading role you are meant to. Surprises are part of your life. Allow yourself to be guided by this invisible force—as you too wield an invisible, magical influence on others.

Master Number 22

You are the Master Architect of PEACE. You manifest achievement and build your dreams into reality. You work hard and embody the power of the Buddha Principle. Your work encompasses spiritual self-study, spiritual self-discipline and spiritual honesty.

As a 22, you are...

- Able to download higher divine wisdom into physical reality

- Designed to build a project/business/idea from the ground up with lasting results

- A Master at invoking Peace and Calm in daily life

To create peaceful solutions and manifest results with lasting impact, you need to be highly disciplined. At times you might feel like you are inferior or don't have all the internal tools necessary. This false belief will propel you to rely too much on outside sources or people's opinions for approval. Understand that you are here as a Master Number 22 to rely on your own abilities—which requires tremendous inner strength. To be a master of manifestation you need patience and strong vigilance to stay "on track."

Without consistent monitoring of your actions, done with full integrity and honesty, you may get blinded by negative actions of people around you that will lead to delusion and frustration. You will experience illusion instead of inner illumination.

Master Numbers ask more of you—they also give you the tools to accomplish more! So use your ability to DISCERN Truth from illusion. Slay the dragons of fear and nebulous energy and replace them with the magnificent light of Truth.

Recognize your spiritual mastery—reflected in how you take responsibility, in spiritual acceptance of how life shows up for you. Practice this spiritual responsibility in your daily life, in your relationships, and to accomplish your goals. Remember that the roles other people play in your life are for multitude reasons—including showing you what NOT to do! This is just as valid a lesson as the person who inspires you as a positive role model. Accepting all experiences and relationships as valid and useful in some way is the key to helping you to the inertia to inner change you can encounter. Some situations or individuals are so challenging that you will make major shifts that result in life-changing readjustments and end up wielding a positive impact on you. Others will refine your sensitivity, propelling you to step into a new role in uplifting society.

Thus, if you refrain from inner growth by avoiding pain, you can miss out on developing an incredibly profound understanding of Peace. The basics surrounding the question and answer to what constitutes a life of peace, are there for you to unlock in your soul. You know that there is a necessary process that we as human beings need to experience to create that inner transformation from ego self to spiritual being, and that this awakening comes as a result of self-awareness and self acceptance. You understand that when we become adults we must move into self-realization, not rely on others to replace our parents' previous guidance. In the same way it is important for you not to be caught up in fads, the latest trends and keeping up with your friends or neighbors in an attempt for outside approval. Conformity is the shadow side of 22/4. Being independent and free to create your OWN order based on your own truth and accepting the consequences of your actions as feedback from the universe (not judgment) is vital to your peace and well-being.

When you are out of alignment you can succumb to indifference, being aimless, reckless, apathetic, self-important, frustrated. You may resent a lack of recognition, be envious of other's successes and exaggerate.

Any area you pursue will allow you to achieve a position of distinction because you are not afraid of challenges, and see them as necessary, even welcome, stepping stones to success. Master Numbers carry majesty and greatness, and your expression of that power comes through your capacity to manifest by planning great projects which you direct into existence (rather than manage the intricacies—you must leave the trivial matters to others). As the "Architect of Peace" Master Number you always want to be at peace with your work and values so you can also enjoy the benefits of the power bestowed on you. Guard against using your ambition to manifest only for personal profit without caring HOW you arrive at your goals.

Master Number 33

You embody the Selfless GIVER and the Cosmic GUARD-
IAN. Others look to you as an example. You have to discern between matyrdom and compassionate service.

As a 33, you are...

- Highly sensitive and could be a powerful Empath

- Designed to be a teacher of Compassion

- Concerned for the welfare of the masses

When expressed at its highest vibrational alignment
Master Number 33 symbolizes a person who embodies
Unconditional Love. 33 carries all the qualities of its root
number 6, yet is even more sensitive—FEELING people's
emotions as deeply as their own. This is the kind of love
that says to anyone who crosses your path, "I accept you
and love you no matter what you do or don't do."

This unconditional love is extended to YOU as well. When
the time comes and you are at the point of transitioning
to another dimension, you will only remember whether
you have been of service and loved to the fullest extent
possible. Nothing else will matter than having led a life
of meaning and a life of love. Service and compassion
create our most profound experiences of love and joy.
And 33/6 encompasses the gamut of this underlying
yearning for human beings to serve and love one another.

To tune into the depths of heart-centered connection required for this level of compassion, there are times when you may experience great doubt or distress, delusion and disappointment in your life. There are many responsibilities a 33/6 Master Number person takes on to understand how to consistently activate the deep empathy of this powerful vibration.

You may struggle with issues of intimacy and loyalty. Putting yourself in a loved one's shoes is integral to your emotional growth. This means looking in the mirror and reflecting on how your words impact others, how your actions impress everyone affected. You also can have a tendency for being a perfectionist, and you must learn to forgive others for not measuring up, beginning first with forgiving yourself for being imperfect (a perfectly natural state to be!).

You are here to uplift others through unconditional loving service and joy, embodying the EMPATH, unpretentious and concerned only with the welfare of all—a teacher of balance and harmony who leads others by example.

When you are out of alignment you can succumb to criticism of self and others, pretentiousness, perfectionism, irresponsibility, setting no clear boundaries, resist reflection, worry, insensitivity, anxiousness, rigid in your beliefs, abuse of power, using money to control.

33/6 comprises two of three numbers in the 3-6-9 Creation triad. You are extraordinarily intuitive and can use your gifts in artistic and creative endeavors. With your supreme appreciation of beauty your sense of aesthetics are exceptional and you can master music, artistic line, color, creative movement and/or form to the highest degree.

Master Number 44

You embody the Practical Visionary and Ingenious Director here to empower others by restoring order and dedication in their life.

As a 44, you are...

- A builder and manifestor of Group Consciousness

- Designed to create new modalities of greater income and abundance

- Trusting of the order of the Universe

You are resourceful and able to manifest valuable ideas in service to others. Your creations are designed to help others rebuild their lives. Your mental abilities are great as is your strength of conviction. 44 exudes a powerful personality which matches their expansive goals. As a 44 you have great magnetism, leadership abilities, powers of persistence and self control. These qualities allow you to reach the highest echelons of power and wealth giving you a great capacity to serve the world.

You are innately practical and strong. Your BIG ideas germinate from an expansive imagination, which can conceive of intricate and grand visions. This ingeniousness allows you to manage and bring together many different aspects of power and personalities—thereby finding seemingly magical solutions to problems others can't solve. You do this by including them in the process, allowing their ideas to blend with the ultimate solution, thereby acting as leader, manager, and magician all at once and bringing complex projects to a harmonious conclusion. This natural genius for directing also stems from your innate ability to analyze and reason while applying compassion and leadership with total confidence and control.

There is a serenity and integrity in you that instantly allows others to feel secure and grounded. You are just, efficient, strong, and ethical—having both tact and an incisive intellect that wields enormous power, as all your energy is poured into making your ideals and ideas REAL.

You do not shy away from work and are tirelessly engaged with your responsibilities and projects, reflecting the self discipline and tenaciousness required for any great leader or organizer. Like all the Master Number vibrations 44 also requires high ideals and complete integrity to be of service. Your great desire is to improve people's lives, and you use your influence, power and fortune to manifest all levels of improvements and elevation in your community.

When you are out of alignment you become inconsiderate, overworked and overstressed, you use money to control others, expect others to manifest your good ideas, have no personal discipline, are critical behind the scenes and envious of others' success, resist responsibility and are dominated by your own ambitions.

As a 44, you use discipline, humility, perseverance, and total dedication to stay on your soul's chosen path. Often your satisfaction for having completed a goal brings the greatest fulfillment—you know that you have prepared for this moment, this life, and the satisfaction of completion is superior to any other reward you may receive.

Master Number 55

When your Destiny Number is 55, your life is reflected by great, fundamental changes. You are a Freedom Seeker and embody Double Intelligence, indicated by your openness and willingness to be adaptable under all conditions.

As a 55, you are...

- Adaptable to change

- Designed to consistently free your mind of rigid, outdated thought patterns

- Able to pivot easily in order generate an internal shift in yourself and help others do the same

It is of vital importance that you don't mistake minor changes for true, fundamental shifts. You vibrate to adventure—initiating risk as an instrument of creation. Thus you are a creative force on every level. You always need to propel your energy into new directions—with the goal of bringing about fundamental change.

Master Number 66

When your Destiny Number is 66, your life is imbued with Double Creative Power and a Voice that needs to heard while being of service to others. This can be in any realms of self expression, from the arts and music to writing or speaking. Your double 6 makes you a cosmic parent to all and allows your heart and soul to approach every action, word and thought with utmost empathy and compassion. You empower others with your loving and supportive words and beautiful message.

As a 66, you are...

- Able to easily step into your responsibilities

- Designed to nurture since you embody Mastery of the Mother/Father Principle

- Able to help Transform other people's emotional state through Joy and Gratitude

As a natural Intuitive you need to surrender to the subconscious realms. This allows you to come home to love. When you are out of alignment you will become oblivious of the spiritual realms and ignore your intuition and responsibilities—even embracing victimization instead of spiritual victory. Be aware that the strength of any master number will be reflected in both the negative and positive expression of its meaning.

Master Number 77

Your life is filled with double Spiritual Insight and Psychic abilities. This is a vibration of transcendence, and those whose full birth certificate names resonate to it will transcend all obstacles through surrender to the Light. You are here to uplift and inspire many! You channel change in mystical ways... often unbeknownst to you, as the energy aligned with 77 is the double lightning strike from heaven to Earth—a shift that bubbles up in your conscious awareness miraculously. You have the gift of tuning in to your Spiritual Guides and the Angelic Realm without even being aware of your connection. 77 represents double intelligence and inventiveness allowing you to reach great heights of spiritual wisdom.

As a 77, you are...

- Able to penetrate straight into the core of any matter

- Designed to release others from mental and spiritual pain

- Able to share your intelligence with those who are afraid to take risks, so their courage bubbles up inside of them and they are energetically brought back into balance

Your ability to focus is acute and your understanding of the psychological state of human nature great. You can "sell" and inspire from the stage, are media savvy and embody fearless expression and joy. You also have a strong interest in mystical secrets.

Master Number 88

When your Destiny Number resonates to 88, your life is one of incredible leadership and the ability to overcome seemingly insurmountable obstacles and gain strength as a result. This is the Master Executive who leads with a profound vision. You embody dignity and excellence to the nines, love going beyond perceived limits and thus symbolize the human version of infinite possibilities—limitlessness.

As a 88, you are...

• Able to Manifest Anything

• Designed to determine the outcome of your future by using the intense force of your creative imagination

• Able to successfully own every facet of your life to the nth degree by directing natural spiritual laws

You are the Abundant One and feel like God's Gift—this 88 Master Number also signifies taking on major responsibilities as a trailblazer.

Master Number 99

When your Destiny Number resonates to 99, your life embodies the qualities of Fulfillment through Unconditional Love. All answers and wisdom are contained within you. You are accomplished and have the answer for pretty much anything. Your abilities can create fortunes.

As a 99, you are...

- Knowledgeable of everything and adept at answering most questions

- Designed to Give—your life is dedicated to helping causes and uplifting humanity

- A supreme leader who leads by example exhibiting the highest integrity and wisdom

You are poetic, romantic, and compassionate—and this allows you to comfort others by your presence. In your highest expression, you can transcend the Ego and merge with Unconditional Love.

CHAPTER 5

DOUBLE DIGIT NUMBERS 10–98

NOW WE WILL DISCOVER THE MEANINGS FOR DOUBLE DIGIT NUMBERS 10 THROUGH 98.
Aside from the double digit "Master Numbers," we have numbers 10 through 98 to explore! When your Life Purpose, Day of Birth, or Destiny Number adds up to a double digit (most do!) you discover additional unique traits, talents, and intensifications that provide deeper insights into who you are at Soul-level. Let's discover the special gifts revealed in your special double-digit vibrations.

Numbers 10–19

NUMBER 10

10 means you can manifest ideas, thoughts, goals, emotions easily and often instantly. That's a big responsibility, so view things optimistically as often as possible. The "0" in 10 adds an element of divine protection. 10 gives you direct access to cosmic wisdom. Dedicate your life to creating Love and Light in all ways, and you will manifest magical outcomes.

The shadow side of number 10 is expressed when you are out of alignment. When you are fixed and inflexible, opinionated, stubborn or prone to exaggeration. You can also become tyrannical if your spiritual awakening and quest for awareness are being neglected.

NUMBER 11 (SEE CHAPTER 4)

NUMBER 12

You have selected a life of service. You are highly creative, affectionate, and loving. You're invested in education, but you may need to give up something to achieve the wisdom you seek. Look within when seeking a solution. By expanding your spiritual and intuitive education, you will reap success and experience happiness.

The shadow side of number 12 is expressed when you are out of alignment. You feel like you are a victim (or victimizing others), sacrificing your life to the point where you've compromised your mission or values to be in servitude to another person or cause, or you've given up your sovereignty, are a doormat or feeling bitter.

NUMBER 13

You experience many changes meant to transform and empower you. You have an "out-of-the-box" approach to life. You can attract sudden changes that are meant to keep you alert and aware. Birth, life, death, and rebirth is a consistent theme. You can access the seen and unseen worlds, manifesting and building innovative projects in both.

The shadow side of number 13 is expressed when you are out of alignment. You focus too much energy on the material at the expense of your spiritual nature. You may participate in destructive actions or over-powering behavior towards others. Your impatience and temper can flare up and suddenly destroy what you have so easily built.

NUMBER 14

14 imbues you with the ability to connect and share information on any platform. You are full of ideas, with a vivid imagination and great energy. You like excitement and motion, yet must stay on the positive expression of your number in order not to feel unstable.

The shadow side of number 14 is expressed when you are out of alignment. You are distractible, stressed, over analytical, neglectful of responsibilities or feel unstable. You can experience both temporary gains and losses, so don't rely on others, but turn to your intuition, your inner communicator, for advice.

NUMBER 15

You have great magnetism and carry enchantment in everything you do. You are aligned with music, drama, and/or art. When you are positively aligned, you attract prosperity and people who help you. Your main mission is to uplift others by blessing them with happiness. You are not afraid of working for your goals. You persevere and have a strong will and convictions.

The shadow side of number 15 is expressed when you are out of alignment. You can step on people's toes, be overbearing, or be curious to the point of nosiness. You also may sacrifice your own needs by helping others, or be indecisive. With this number you must always focus your intention on the highest good for all.

NUMBER 16

Your intuition will warn you of unexpected changes and even danger—whether through dreams or your gut feelings. Perfect your intuitive hunches; ignoring them can attract challenges. You work best alone. That's when you receive powerful and sudden illuminations. You like to feel empowered. You also prefer quality over quantity.

It is important for you to learn about being faithful and honest, so be guarded against promiscuity and unfaithfulness. Other shadow side expressions are impatience, over analyzing, being impulsive or reckless. A tyrannical side or using words or actions in an abusive way are extreme negative expressions of this vibration.

NUMBER 17

You will leave behind a legacy—to your family, community, or the greater world. You are attracted to exploring and making visible hidden mysteries of the universe. You also want to help create peace and love for humankind. You may have had challenges earlier in life, which you overcome later; you have a survivor's mindset and resilience.

Your challenge in life is to achieve a high degree of detachment, to understand that power and influence are only to be used for the benefit of uplifting others. You may be stubborn, pessimistic, and lose complete faith with where the world is heading. These doubts can create a superficial quality.

NUMBER 18

18 loves to dream and requires time to rest. Your creativity and compassion coupled with your natural charisma can make you a leader. You have the capability to build empires. You are sensitive to the rhythms of life. Sometimes this high sensitivity turns into a nervous energy, so it is important for you to meditate and chill regularly.

You either lead by inspiring others—or you can mislead and be used as an example of what not to do. So, you may use your power for the sake of ego-gratification. You may be touchy, easily irritated, deceived by others, not aware of close dangers, consciously profit from conflict or in a state of conflict about spirituality and materialism.

NUMBER 19

You may attract many changes and shifts in your life that require you to start from scratch. You attract others into your energy field. You have a wonderful creativity, which may be accompanied by equally strong insecurities. Believe in yourself and stand on your own two feet to reach true happiness and peace.

The shadow side of number 19 is expressed when you are out of alignment. You feel insecure and lack the confidence to make a decision, or turn to self-pity. You might get impulsive and impatient. You like to keep your secrets close and may turn to deceit, even going so far as experiencing a "fall" from grace.

Numbers 20–29

NUMBER 20

You will experience a powerful awakening, bringing new purpose and goals. The "0" in 20 adds an element of divine protection. You may find success in life as part of a team. You work well with groups and can create harmony. The choices you make bring tests. You are constantly adapting and renewing.

The shadow side of number 20 is expressed when you are out of alignment. You are resentful, exhibit uncontrolled emotions, identify as being weak, are easily disillusioned, feel separate from the world, resist change and are uncooperative or undiplomatic in your communication style.

NUMBER 21

You are here to help set everyone free from what is not real. You are a highly creative, versatile and well-rounded person and can express yourself through any modality, career, form, or material. Address any self-doubt; you will develop sound confidence and be grateful and generous to all of life and everyone you meet.

The shadow side of number 21 is expressed when you are out of alignment. You fear rejection, become overly critical, you dissipate your gifts with frivolous activities, you resort to lying, your insecurities result in self-centeredness

NUMBER 22 (SEE CHAPTER 4)

NUMBER 23

You have the desire for freedom and want to explore and enjoy life to the fullest. Your strength lies in your ideas and intelligence. You have a quick mind, a great memory, and the ability to learn easily. You also have the confidence to manifest your ideas. Communication and research come naturally to you. 23 is an ambitious and courageous vibration. You are loyal and passionate.

The shadow side of number 23 is expressed when you are out of alignment. You act hastily, are headstrong with quick outbursts of temper, you are impatient, self-centered and patronizing of others

NUMBER 24

Once you realize how you can serve others with passion and joy, you can easily attract abundance and nurturing relationships. Your success is supported by others. You are a loving, lively companion. You take responsibility for your life and goals. Your dreams nurture your soul and uplift others. You want to live in abundance and beauty.

The shadow side of number 24 is expressed when you are out of alignment. You easily become jealous, you are domineering and controlling—interfering in other people's lives, unfaithful and put too much pressure on yourself to the point of sacrifice.

NUMBER 25

You are a thinker and an idealist who is selective, analytical, and scientific. You need peace and quiet and tend to be reserved. People look up to you for your knowledge and wisdom. You are adept at observation. 25 can be a spiritual crusader. You learn from past mistakes. You must have great respect for your partner.

With your need for privacy, you can be secretive and hard to get to know. It can be a real challenge sharing your feelings. Notice when you feel internal conflict—it will dissipate your energy. Guard against starting something and not following through. When totally out of alignment, you can resort to cruelty.

NUMBER 26

A natural leader, you excel in business, money matters, and management. You have endurance and stamina. You understand the material/physical world. You are not a detail-oriented person—your overall vision inspires and nourishes you. Due to your high standards, you can do almost anything well. You are generous.

The shadow side of number 26 is expressed when you are out of alignment. You can be impulsive and impatient. You don't spend enough time on your personal relationships—which can lead to a disorganized personal life. Guard against craving too much power, and materialism.

NUMBER 27

You exude a sense of excellence and authority blended with a humanitarian spirit. 27 is a vibration of courage, love, compassion and wise leadership. You love to share and uplift, and you do so without expecting anything in return. Focus on your own creative ideas and don't listen to those who differ with your internal compass.

The shadow side of number 27 is expressed when you are out of alignment. You can get indecisive and confused. When others don't measure up to your idea of perfection you become intolerant. Your perfectionist standards can make you critical.

NUMBER 28

You have an original approach to life and unique, inventive ideas. This makes you want to explore life to the fullest and ignites your ambitious nature. You innately "remember" who you are at soul level and are here to remind others of that eternal connection. Everything that happens to you is a reminder of your true origin.

The shadow side of number 28 is expressed when you are out of alignment. You can get indecisive and confused. When others don't measure up to your idea of perfection you become intolerant. Your perfectionist standards can make you critical.

NUMBER 29

You are here to develop faith in your gifts and trust in the goodness of your Soul. You take your life and role seriously. When you honor yourself as an individualist—a creator of original ideas and visions—your trust in goodness creates healing. You have high standards. You are a leader and teacher of wisdom.

You can be fearful and uncertain, resulting in division and indecision running through your life. You may attract unreliable friends, trust too easily and get anxious easily around others—especially members of the opposite sex. Your anxiety can lead to "feeling frozen" and stubbornness.

Numbers 30–39

NUMBER 30

You are artistic. Express your feelings through words or creative projects; you will inspire others too. You have a strong mind. Though you are easygoing and warm socially, you need your alone time, which allows you to nurture your talent. You take chances and need beautiful surroundings. 30 is here to uplift and celebrate.

The shadow side of number 30 is expressed when you are out of alignment. You can be impulsive and impatient. You don't spend enough time on your personal relationships—which can lead to a disorganized personal life. Guard against craving too much power or being overly materialistic.

NUMBER 31

31 signifies genius and out-of-the-box thinking. You are determined, but you need time alone to make your ideas real. You have a natural retrospection. You like to be self-sufficient and need your own space—which will allow you turn your ideas into results. You want security, though not at the expense of personal freedom.

The shadow side of number 31 is expressed when you are out of alignment. You can get nervous and isolate yourself, becoming a recluse and poverty-conscious. Any loneliness is a sign that you need to confront lingering anger issues, resentment or misunderstandings. Guard against overwork and being disorganized.

NUMBER 32

32 stands for freedom and connection to people, especially through magnetic presence or speech. You have
a natural charm. Your message tends to be about good
visions for the future. You are like a warrior, activating
both your sense of responsibility and what is for everyone's highest good.

The shadow side of number 32 is expressed when you
are out of alignment. You only live for the adrenaline rush
and excitement. You may be high-strung. You can resort
to overanalyzing, impulsiveness, and impatience. You
may easily give up. You can feel superior over others
and proud.

NUMBER 33 (SEE CHAPTER 4)

NUMBER 34

34 governs order, steady growth, and a patient approach
to manifesting your goals. You are attracted to the hidden mysteries of life. You have a way of combining the
creative in an organized way to elevate your understanding and mindset. You learn from the past well. You are a
quick thinker, an excellent planner, and logical.

The shadow side of number 34 is expressed when you
are out of alignment. You can get impulsive and impatient. You may talk too much. You may use violent tactics
to get what you want.

NUMBER 35

Creating wealth, position, and power are your main goals. The energy exchange of money fascinates you. You are recognized for work well done. You are generous, affectionate, charming, and fully engaged in your independence. You are on an ultimate adventure to find the true meaning of prosperity. You have large energy reserves.

You can be judgmental and self-indulgent. You may have false beliefs about money by imposing a negative mindset on abundance, when money is a tool—here to be understood and used to make a positive change. You may be unreasonable and unpredictable as well as undisciplined.

NUMBER 36

You are here to live in alignment with your heart center. Implementing your true mission will enable you to step fully into the life you were born to live. You must use the energy in your inspirations and inventions for good. You are dependable and honest. Use your deep acceptance of truth to overcome doubts. Your creations can be genius.

The shadow side of number 36 is expressed when you are out of alignment. You may experience cycles of ups and downs which lead to imbalance. You may act in haste, before thinking. You may be emotionally distant due to your great sensitivity. You can be concerned about completions and endings.

NUMBER 37

You are sensitive, private, and deeply spiritual. You tend to have good friendships, love, and romance. Partnerships in general are good for you, both business and personal. You have a magnetic relationship with the public—especially in the arts. You are wise in how you express your emotions.

The shadow side of number 37 is expressed when you are out of alignment. You may be dishonest, deceitful or manipulative. You may not trust your intuition and turn to others for answers. Guard against emotional conflicts. You can get aggressive.

NUMBER 38

You are highly intuitive and attuned to the divine. You trust in that bridge between your conscious and un-conscious, connecting to the unseen. This is a number of natural clairvoyance. You are happiest when being in service to others. Your energy field can sometimes be larger than average. You are an instrument of wisdom and peace.

The shadow side of number 38 is expressed when you are out of alignment. You may lack a connection to your spiritual nature, have emotional and physical challenges due to blocked creativity, live extravagantly (beyond your means), be immoral, and use deception. You may get paranoid and have phobias.

NUMBER 39

You are gentle and love humanity. Making the world a kinder, gentler, better place is one of your visions. You must live and create in peace and contentment. You love to learn and are philosophical. You can tap into both your mind and heart. Your life feels smooth and happy when you speak with feeling and vulnerability.

The shadow side of number 39 is expressed when you are out of alignment. You may over-indulge in the sensual. You can be insensitive to others or get lazy or be easily distracted. If life feels like a drama or you resort to exaggeration or lies, it is a sign that you are creatively unfulfilled.

Numbers 40–49

NUMBER 40

You are dedicated to following a strategy or plan of action and will persevere until each project is fully completed. This sense of order and structure makes you feel at ease and happy. You also carry an entrepreneurial streak and are a natural at managing others. You demand a lot from others and yourself. You are a natural peacemaker.

The shadow side of number 40 is expressed when you are out of alignment. You may have a negative disposition which leads to pessimism and confusion. You can see life as a series of obstacles. You may be undisciplined and unreliable. You can chase goals that are illusions and squander money.

NUMBER 41

You have an open and flexible approach to life, giving you the ability to bounce back quickly from challenges, which don't leave a long and strong impact on you. Being authentic will give you openness and freedom in any relationship. Your feelings and senses are filled with enthusiasm, a pioneering spirit, and wonderful versatility.

The shadow side of number 41 is expressed when you are out of alignment. You may be resistant to change and inflexible in your attitude. You can feel timid and afraid to take on responsibility. You may be impulsive and lose ground when you act too quickly. Guard against over-indulgence.

NUMBER 42

Your deepest intention is to love and to be loved. People appreciate you and the compassion you share, and they are willing to go the distance to keep you close. Your home must feel beautiful and exude warmth. You need an outlet for your creativity, which may be inspired by visions. You are charming, charismatic, and generous.

The shadow side of number 42 is expressed when you are out of alignment. You can be selfish and think you're here to save the world. You may feel misunderstood, neglected, or unappreciated. You can feel overburdened. You can be dishonest and irresponsible.

NUMBER 43

43 symbolizes a strong intuition—when everything is in flow and your mind is clear. You are practical, creative, and strong, both in the physical and spiritual realms. 43 can also symbolize revolution. Your biggest break-throughs come when you are by yourself, or alone in nature. You can attract happy endings and plenty into your life.

The shadow side of number 43 is expressed when you are out of alignment. You can experience emotional and physical pain due to excess. You can feel isolated, angry, or conflicted. You enjoy wielding power.

NUMBER 44 (SEE CHAPTER 4)

NUMBER 45

4 gives you a firm foundation—the Great Pyramid sits on a perfect four-sided square. 5 lets you communicate and experience freedom of movement, and the root number 9 holds the wisdom and love of the previous single digits. This combination gives you a magnetic energy. You are a born humanitarian, merging independence with discipline.

The shadow side of number 45 is expressed when you are out of alignment. At times your practicality of your ideas with be in conflict. You may be regretful and discouraged. If you brood over the past and any lost opportunities, you can feel gloomy. You may come across as egotistical and proud.

NUMBER 46

Others see you as intensely motivated and independent. You embody passion turned into action, with the discipline, creativity, and compassion to make an impact. It is your role to take the lead. You are well-rounded and able to delegate, guiding others to manifest your ideas. Your intuitive abilities may also birth new inventions.

The shadow side of number 46 is expressed when you are out of alignment. You may be childish and irresponsible. You can take advantage of those who admire you. You may be self-centered and thoughtless. At times you may resort to judging or even condemning others. Guard against pride and not being able to forgive.

NUMBER 47

Having specific, inspiring goals is important to your success. Your charm and magnetism will help you fulfill your dreams. You have much to give, which instills confidence. Mundane work won't make you happy. Discern what is important; discard what is not. This daily balance is crucial for your peace of mind and abundance.

The shadow side of number 47 is expressed when you are out of alignment. You do not discern and are indecisive, which dissipates your energy. You may succumb to distractions and temptations which take you away from your purpose. You may latch on to delusions—or get too emotional.

NUMBER 48

You crave freedom of speech and movement. You focus on attaining higher knowledge, and you enjoy expanding your understanding by traveling the world. You are a logical thinker focused on manifestation and the belief that there is plenty to go around. You thrive in the arts or creative problem solving. Focus on one passion and commit fully.

The shadow side of number 48 is expressed when you are out of alignment. You may get moody and blocked creatively. You can be cynical and intolerant. You may feel too sensitive. If you turn away from the spiritual, you will not find fulfillment.

NUMBER 49

Your compassion and brilliant ideas blend into outcomes that will benefit many. Your gifts are rooted in your integrity, intuition, executive skills, and attention to justice. Financial success is assured when you apply them. You are patient, honest, and diplomatic. You know when it is important to wait. You are also loyal and affectionate.

The shadow side of number 49 is expressed when you are out of alignment. You may have no drive to succeed and resort to greed or excess. You may fear taking risks or be afraid of change. You can distrust the unknown, unseen, and spiritual and hesitate, thereby losing an opportunity.

Numbers 50–59

NUMBER 50

5 blends your quest for freedom and joy. Your life is filled with movement, achievement, and a quest for adventure. You may be drawn to serve in a public way to make the world a better place. With your magnetism and persuasion powers, you are also a master at "selling" what you are passionate about. Your imagination is great.

The shadow side of number 50 is expressed when you are out of alignment. You can feel frazzled and overwhelmed. You may be irresponsible and wasteful while easily getting distracted. You may not complete projects that you started and be indecisive.

NUMBER 51

You have a strong intelligence enhanced by your deep perception and gifts of discernment. This enables you to make sound judgments, which you base on facts balanced with compassion. You are filled with helpful ideas and have an active mind; you are an innovator and visionary to the highest degree.

The shadow side of number 51 is expressed when you are out of alignment. You can be narrow-minded and bigoted as you drive for total power. You may be cruel to others or harsh on yourself. You might attract intense rivalries. You can be too stoic and stern.

NUMBER 52

52 is a powerfully sacred vibration and brings an enormous appetite to learn mystical secrets and explore the unknown. You need to understand the link between the seen and unseen worlds. Your wisdom and confidence is great, making you stand out from the crowd.

The shadow side of number 52 is expressed when you are out of alignment. Guard against narrow-mindedness and jealousy. You can shut the door to the outside world due to an inability to handle noise or distractions. You may feel separated from Source.

NUMBER 53

53 is a leadership number, so it is best that you work for yourself. You are oriented towards financial abundance and business; you would thrive in a field that utilizes your gifts of invention. You are creative, free, verbal, and inquisitive. You can accomplish a lot even with obstacles. You have a deep feeling that there is much to do.

The shadow side of number 53 is expressed when you are out of alignment. You may be aggressive, exhibit and air of cockiness, and be quick to fight. You like being alone and need to learn to share as well.

NUMBER 54

54 balances the qualities of freedom and discipline. So there must be an equal distribution between work and play, having a plan and being free to explore. This makes you more of an idealist or dreamer, at times.

The shadow side of number 54 is expressed when you are out of alignment. You may be cynical and not comfortable in your own shoes. Guard against not finishing projects you started.

NUMBER 55 (SEE CHAPTER 4)

NUMBER 56

56 is a highly sensitive number. You need to balance your desire for adventure and freedom with your strong need for love, home, and family. Deep within you, you carry firm convictions that are based on truth and peace. You are charming and popular, loyal and affectionate. This is a very musical vibration.

The shadow side of number 56 is expressed when you are out of alignment. You may be too sensitive and easily overwhelmed or anxious. You can obsessive and nervous. Decisions can be challenging.

NUMBER 57

57 is a blend of intellectual prowess and inventiveness. You are unique in your approach. You express your ideas in beautiful ways. You have high ideals and are charitable.

The shadow side of number 57 is expressed when you are out of alignment. You may feel sorry for yourself, going into victimization mode. You might not be able to see positives. You can be bitter.

NUMBER 58

58 is a vibration of peace and balance. You require a quiet environment to keep your security and stability intact. You are open to getting work done and this facilitates your implementation of projects and goals. You can make lightning quick decisions. You have high standards and self control. You are naturally charming.

The shadow side of number 58 is expressed when you are out of alignment. You can feel stressed and rest poorly. You can be difficult to please. You may be opinionated, stubborn, even dogmatic.

NUMBER 59

You are persuasive and brilliant. You would make a great salesperson or attorney. You feel at ease with anyone, no matter who they are. You thrive anywhere you can use your compassion and wit. You have a sparkle in your eyes.

The shadow side of number 59 is expressed when you are out of alignment. You must learn to discern between what is supportive and positive and what is not. You may risk too much, just to feel alive. Guard against impulsiveness. You must learn when to retreat.

Numbers 60–69

NUMBER 60

60 merges the number of love, service, and compassion with 0, the vibration of divine protection. This is a number of harmony, joy, gratitude, warmth, and pleasure. You are charming, magnetic, wise, artistic, and have a great literary sense. You enjoy traveling for your career. You are responsible and relied upon.

The shadow side of number 60 is expressed when you are out of alignment. You may use knowledge to further negative intentions. You can be rebellious. Guard against selfishness and egotistical behavior. You may serve to the point of being subservient.

NUMBER 61

61 is connected to an intellectual and idealistic approach to life. You have a strong interest in strange phenomena and divination arts. You strive to live a life of achievement and have great potential. Intimate connection can be a challenge for you. This is also a vibration of keeping secrets, great if you work in law or undercover.

The shadow side of number 61 is expressed when you are out of alignment. You can feel uncertain and then hesitate, which can hold you back. You may feel unstable and need to tap into discipline and self-confidence. Be careful not to go into a negative mindset.

NUMBER 62

You are a wonderful caregiver. You can be an excellent health practitioner, healing intuitive, and mentor. You are focused on abundance and have a knack for business and management. You use obstacles as a path to growth, and are skilled at finding solutions.

The shadow side of number 62 is expressed when you are out of alignment. You may encounter health issues. Take note when you feel suppressed or out of sync within your personal relationships.

NUMBER 63

63 is a passionate, creative number. This is a vibration of great strength and compassion. You have a deep desire to uplift the world and create something of value for others. Your artistic abilities are pronounced. Your creativity can take you to a place of genius.

The shadow side of number 63 is expressed when you are out of alignment. You may experience regret when you look back at past experiences. Guard against hopelessness. Your emotions may run too high, or you could be self-conscious and aloof.

NUMBER 64

64 gives you a keen perception and intelligence that arises from the heart-center and translates into manifestation of your ideas. You have a strong will to succeed. You are drawn to literary or creative pursuits. You exude confidence and have a captivating personality.

The shadow side of number 64 is expressed when you are out of alignment. You can be disorganized. Guard against being overly positive. Be sure to spend time developing your spiritual nature and faith in the natural, loving order of the universe. You may resort to fear and identify with suffering.

NUMBER 65

Number 6 imbues you with love and compassion and 5 expresses a yearning for freedom. 65 asks that you balance freedom with family commitments. When your life is in balance all your desires can be fulfilled as this number is aligned with prosperity. You can handle money matters with wisdom and care.

The shadow side of number 65 is expressed when you are out of alignment. You feel self-indulgent and may resort to fulfilling negative intentions. You may be overly sensitive.

NUMBER 66 (SEE CHAPTER 4)

NUMBER 67

You have compassion and intellect. 67 is also connected to the natural order of the universe. Thus it is connected to mathematics, numbers, and inventions. You plan wise moves and are practical. Your persistence allows you to achieve long-lasting results.

The shadow side of number 67 is expressed when you are out of alignment. You can get lazy and irresponsible. You may resort to dogma. Guard against being obsessive or fanatical.

NUMBER 68

68 is great for proclaiming your message and connecting to others with compassionate leadership. You have a broad vision of how to implement your goals. Your sense of humor allows you to break barriers. Love and leadership propel you.

The shadow side of number 68 is expressed when you are out of alignment. You can be introverted. Guard against insensitivity. You may be crafty.

NUMBER 69

69 activates deep, profound loving kindness and responsibility to others. You may sacrifice your life to be of service to a greater cause or message. You want to nurture or teach. You are creative, and your artistic expressions create magic. Sharing your heart unconditionally is your greatest goal.

The shadow side of number 69 is expressed when you are out of alignment. You can put your life on hold and be in servitude instead of in service. You may get obsessed or infatuated by other people or possessions. Guard against greed or corruption.

Numbers 70–79

NUMBER 70

70 is a vibration of change and silence. You are an eccentric and a natural loner and need to spend time in a place of serenity, preferably near nature. Your intuitive downloads create commercial value. You seek to learn the truth and find solutions. You have a desire to make a distinct contribution and to take control of it.

The shadow side of number 70 is expressed when you are out of alignment. You can isolate yourself which can lead to instability. Your fluctuating moods may interrupt your intuitive flow. You may worry too much. Guard against living pretentiously.

NUMBER 71

71 represents your willingness to grow steadily and slowly. You are dynamic and determined. You have great faith and are balanced energetically. You can be a loner—and are not easily distracted. 71 reduces to the root number 8 and governs financial success.

The shadow side of number 71 is expressed when you are out of alignment. You can be lazy and indifferent. Guard against being too much of a loner. You may miss out on opportunities. You can struggle with staying true to your core spiritual values.

NUMBER 72

72 is the number of compassion and artistry. Your intuitive abilities and wisdom are used to bring peace. You have a strong character and are strong in your productivity. You are highly skilled at handling wealth, and a great person to accomplish major projects and endeavors. You have high standards and love to learn.

The shadow side of number 72 is expressed when you are out of alignment. You may be materialistic. You may crave more than you need. Guard against neglecting your spiritual ideals.

NUMBER 73

73 needs to feel versatile and free to express itself creatively. The individualistic nature of this number inspires others. You are creative and affectionate. You love to learn, read and have a wide-ranging imagination. Your confidence results in leadership positions. Always seek inner wisdom.

The shadow side of number 73 is expressed when you are out of alignment. You can be obstinate and demanding. If you are out of alignment financial hardships can result. You may become materialistic.

NUMBER 74

74 carries idealism. You are psychic; pay attention to your dreams and hunches, as they can be premonitions. You must balance the grounding Earth number (4) with the spiritual, intuitive 7. Bringing these qualities together creates the gift of prophecy. You are a teacher and can channel energy.

The shadow side of number 74 is expressed when you are out of alignment. You can be obstinate and demanding. If you are out of alignment financial hardships can result. You may become materialistic.

NUMBER 75

75 channels joyful freedom from a place of serenity. Your spiritual perception inspires you to be adventurous. You are meant to carry the light of limitless opportunities in your heart and mind. Your faith and idealism merge with your curiosity and creativity to manifest intelligent solutions.

The shadow side of number 75 is expressed when you are out of alignment. You may be overly analytical or idealistic. You can run around in circles. Guard against getting caught up in frustration.

NUMBER 76

You can work steadily for long hours at inspiring projects. Work brings you pleasure. You are honest, reliable, and good at planning, managing and organizing. You can turn intuitive insights into physical reality. Change can be a constant in your life, and you embrace these shifts as important growth experiences.

The shadow side of number 76 is expressed when you are out of alignment. You may be dishonest or resort to fraud. Guard against being fanatical.

NUMBER 77 (SEE CHAPTER 4)

NUMBER 78

78 stands for wealth, alchemy, and fulfillment. Your success comes from trusting your inner voice for answers (7) and taking those insights and solutions to create a vision (8). You have a great passion to serve and uplift others. You are magnetic and easy to relate to due to your strong mind, confidence, and compassion.

The shadow side of number 78 is expressed when you are out of alignment. You may be lazy and dissipate your energy. You can easily feel overburdened. You can lose a fortune as easily as you can make it.

NUMBER 79

79 channels wisdom through intuition and is a vibration of high leadership. As a 79 you reflect a keen intelligence which is merged with a deep compassion for humanity. This is a number of royalty and can indicate a position that influences a broad spectrum of mankind.

The shadow side of number 79 is expressed when you are out of alignment. You may be a recluse, and abdicate your mission to lead by example. Guard against being ruthless and self-righteous.

Numbers 80–89

NUMBER 80

80 is a number of executive leadership and business. You are good at holding a vision and leading others. Any position that allows you to delegate and lead will enable you to express your gifts. Entrepreneurship is especially suited to you. This is a vibration of financial abundance and your mind will be focused on attracting prosperity.

The shadow side of number 80 is expressed when you are out of alignment. You can be inflexible and set in your ways. Guard against being aggressive. You may like to be on your own, but sharing is an important lesson for you.

NUMBER 81

81 gives you wisdom and power. You have the leadership number 1 merged with the executive leadership 8 and expressed through compassionate leadership 9. Your role is to help others let go of their emotional blocks and guide them to self-confidence and creativity. You enjoy the luxuries of life and will aspire to manifest abundance.

The shadow side of number 81 is expressed when you are out of alignment. Watch for these clues: You may hide your emotions in order not to share your deepest vulnerabilities. Or you may overreact to defend yourself. Notice when you are not truly listening, or feeling tense, nervous, aimless, or frustrated.

NUMBER 82

82 is another number of leadership. The courage of the 8 is expressed with a great sense of peace and balance. You will have to strike a balance between your career and intimate partnerships. Both contribute to your kind, gentle yet strong and confident character. You are a role model to others.

The shadow side of number 82 is expressed when you are out of alignment. You may lack compassion and be intolerant of others. You can be ruthless in the pursuit of your goals. Guard against wanting to dominate others. Be open to a sharing, equal partnership.

NUMBER 83

83 is an intuitive vibration, though may not be that open about its clairvoyant gifts. You are a channel—making the unseen visible. What you bring into conscious awareness allows you and everyone else to feel strong and confident. This is highly charged leadership number. You have the gift to bring opposing sides into harmony.

The shadow side of number 83 is expressed when you are out of alignment. You may easily get paranoid and can have phobias. You can be insensitive or overly sensitive. You need to protect your intuitive gifts.

NUMBER 84

84 is a powerful vibration of manifestation. You like to plan, build and make your visions concrete and real. Your creativity is a great asset as it allows you to be flexible within a context of discipline and structure. You also have an individualistic streak and can merge the unconventional with the tried and true.

The shadow side of number 84 is expressed when you are out of alignment. You may feel victimized or resort to controlling others. There can be an internal conflict between honoring either your creative and your organized nature—both need to be nurtured at the same time.

NUMBER 85

85 enjoys hard work, if there is a way to incorporate freedom and vision. Due to its willingness to implement goals and plans, this number represents success. Opportunities can come out of nowhere and often the decision-making needs to move quickly. As a leader of freedom and joy, you need to balance pleasure and work.

The shadow side of number 85 is expressed when you are out of alignment. You can have strong opinions and be rigid in your approach to others. You can feel under strain and this leads to not resting well. You can be difficult to please.

NUMBER 86

86 is a vibration of leadership through love. You are invested in helping others tap into their confidence and know how to elevate others through humor and by instilling a sense of responsibility that they can be proud of. You are an instrument of joy. Balance your need for leadership with your need for a loving home life.

The shadow side of number 86 is expressed when you are out of alignment. You can be insensitive to others. Guard against focusing too much on yourself. You may abdicate your responsibilities and overindulge in sensual pleasures.

NUMBER 87

87 brings leadership to a level of magic, as the energetic alchemy you create can turn into a healing experience. You can mesmerize and magnetize. Your charisma and compassion are irresistible and allow you to help facilitate spiritual awakening in others. You thrive with a secure, loving home base. Your creative gifts easily attract abundance.

The shadow side of number 87 is expressed when you are out of alignment. You may struggle to create a balance between the practical and spiritual realms. Your intense passion can turn into obsession. You can give too much and dissipate your core energy resources.

NUMBER 88 (SEE CHAPTER 4)

NUMBER 89

89 is aligned with infinite resources and is comfortable being in the spotlight. You enjoy travel and the accolades that come with leadership. Your confidence is merged with wisdom and love, giving you an air of royalty. Wealth is attracted to you and you yearn to leave behind a legacy. You have a unique perspective on life.

The shadow side of number 89 is expressed when you are out of alignment. You tend to need to be admired and feel lost without consistent accolades and praise. Understand that power and influence are only to be used for the benefit of uplifting others. You may be stubborn and pessimistic.

Numbers 90–98

NUMBER 90

90 is a number of the wise leader, who dedicates his or her life to bettering the state of humanity. This number brings a strong sense commitment towards inspiring others. Your objective is always to bring positive energy to all endeavors and people. Love and wisdom shared with courage and humility are the main themes.

The shadow side of number 90 is expressed when you are out of alignment. You may be so caught up being a messenger that you become aloof and removed from others. Your ego may be greatly inflated, signifying the image of the number 9 with a big head at the top.

NUMBER 91

91 is a combination of endings and beginnings, bringing the power to shift and create new experiences that reboot and repower others. 91 is a creative number and brings tremendous manifestation abilities. You are driven to lead by example, carve your place in the world, and create success. You have an out-of-the-box approach to life.

The shadow side of number 91 is expressed when you are out of alignment. You can be opinionated and stubborn. You may isolate yourself. Guard against wanting to dominate others.

NUMBER 92

You take your life and role seriously. When you honor yourself as an individualist—a creator of original ideas and visions—you create miraculous healing. You balance love and intimacy, compassion and cooperation in all you do. As a wise leader, you set an example for peace. You have a mission to help and support humanity.

The shadow side of number 92 is expressed when you are out of alignment. You can have division and indecision running through your life. You may trust too easily and get anxious around others. You have to protect yourself against those who don't wish you well, due to your high sensitivity.

NUMBER 93

You are intuitive and need outlets to express your feelings. You want to use your creativity serve others. You must live in a place of peace and contentment. You love to learn and are philosophical. Your life feels smooth and happy when you embrace your ability to speak with feeling and vulnerability—not just from the mind.

The shadow side of number 93 is expressed when you are out of alignment. You can be insensitive to others or get lazy or be easily distracted. If life feels like a drama or you resort to exaggeration or lies, it is a sign that you are creatively unfulfilled. You may have difficulty committing to projects or partnerships.

NUMBER 94

94 creates a strong urge to manifest wisdom and love. You want practically implemented compassion and are affectionate. You need a stable, secure home base, though your growth is tied to surprises. You have gifts in integrity, intuition, executive skills, and attention to justice. You are patient, loyal, honest, and diplomatic.

The shadow side of number 94 is expressed when you are out of alignment. You are not that comfortable with change. You may fear taking risks, or be afraid of change. You can distrust the unknown, unseen, and spiritual and hesitate, thereby loosing an opportunity.

NUMBER 95

You love movement and travel, and your quest for independence governs all you do. Though you are not practical in how you manifest your humanitarian nature, your ability to reach people bypasses most challenges and you can implement your vision. You thrive on variety; you use your compassion and quick wit to tackle any situation.

The shadow side of number 95 is expressed when you are out of alignment. You may have goals that are too idealistic. You must learn to discern between what is supportive and positive and what is not. Guard against impulsiveness and jumping into action too quickly.

NUMBER 96

96 is a powerful vibration of unconditional love, compassion, and alchemy. Your kind nature focuses on those you care about. You have a mission to uplift everyone through joy and change their lives with the magic of a smile. You are artistic and creative. To share your heart lovingly and unconditionally is your greatest mission.

The shadow side of number 96 is expressed when you are out of alignment. You may sacrifice too much of yourself for others or a cause. Guard against not taking care of your own needs at the expense of serving others. You may be greedy or corrupt.

NUMBER 97

97 is a vibration of the spiritual channel of unconditional love. You need quiet due to your internal serenity. A calm environment and close vicinity to nature help you to channel wisdom. You reflect intelligence, which is merged with your compassion for humanity. 97 can indicate a position that influences a broad spectrum of mankind.

The shadow side of number 97 is expressed when you are out of alignment. You may be too sensitive and shut yourself off—become reclusive. You may abdicate your mission to lead by example, showing the way to utilize intuition in all parts of life. Guard against being self-righteous.

NUMBER 98

98 is an idealistic vibration and represents leadership through love. You care about abundance and the importance of giving everyone tools for prosperity. Your quest for financial security inspires others. Your confidence is merged with wisdom and love. You yearn to leave behind a legacy. You have a unique perspective on life.

The shadow side of number 98 is expressed when you are out of alignment. You are highly sensitive and may have a challenging time sharing your true feelings. You can come across as aloof. Understand that power and influence are only to be used for the benefit of uplifting others. You may be stubborn and pessimistic.

NUMBER 99 (SEE CHAPTER 4)

CHAPTER 6

PERSONAL YEAR, MONTH, AND DAYS AND YOUR POWER CYCLES

NOW THAT YOU HAVE A GOOD PERSPECTIVE ON YOUR SOUL BIRTH BLUEPRINT, IT'S TIME TO MOVE INTO PRESENT-TIME! Your birthday started a continuous series of personal cycles that measure and describe the active energies influencing your life—energies you can fully take advantage of! By knowing the meaning and timing of your personal year, month and day vibrations, you have a powerful tool to take your life from good to great.

In this chapter, you'll discover how to calculate your cycles. You'll also be able to see which of your Personal Years, Days, and Months are Power Cycles. These will intensify the energy and attract experiences and opportunities that lead to even greater growth and overall advancement.

The Three Important Numbers in Your Personal Cycles

Your current and future cycles are comprised of:

1. Your **Personal Year**—the vibration you are experiencing from one birthday to the next birthday

2. Your **Personal Month**—each calendar month carries a specific personal vibration for you

3. Your **Personal Day**—every day carries a specific personal vibration for you

Your personal cycles are an invitation to consciously participate in creating your reality in the most optimal way possible. Once you get into the rhythm of your yearly, monthly and daily cycles, you hold the keys to the natural ebb and flow of your life in full alignment with your Soul Blueprint.

How to Calculate Your Personal YEARS

Let's begin with your Personal Year vibration. Some numerologists start *everyone's* Personal Year on January 1. However, I have found with reading thousands of clients that the shift we feel on New Year's day is related to the *Universal Year* Number changing, not our individual Personal Year. You see, there are Universal cycles which impacts everyone collectively, and then your personal cycles which are totally unique to you. When the Universal Year number shifts every January 1, we all feel the change. But your Personal Year begins on your Birthday, not on January 1.

Astrology too focuses on the shift on your birthday. It is always on your birthday that your Solar Return astrology chart is created (when the Sun returns to its exact position that it was at the moment of your birth), to give you the energetic forecast of your next year—not on January 1.

When you consider that the day you were born began your life, gave you your Life Purpose Number (which was your first Personal Year on Earth!), then it makes total sense to begin your next vibrational cycle at the same time on your birthday every year. Besides, that's the day your age changes too!

Your Personal Year begins in the Month of your Birthday. You change your AGE and your Personal Year on your BIRTHDAY, not on January 1. So for a birthday in June, your Personal Year (and your age) begins in June of one year, and runs until May the following year.

This means that within one Calendar Year, a person born during any month except January would experience TWO different Personal Year Numbers:

1. One carried over from the previous calendar year UNTIL their birthday.

2. One FROM their birthday month onwards.

Your current Personal Year is derived by adding the digits of your Day of Birth and Month of Birth to the current calendar year and reducing to a single digit. Every new personal year begins the month that you were born in. Your next Personal Year Number will be one digit lower, unless you're currently in a 9 Personal Year, in which case your next Personal Year will be 1.

Let's look at some examples.

IF YOU WERE BORN		AND THE YEAR IS	YOUR PERSONAL YEAR IS		AND IT RUNS
MAY	23	2019			MAY 2019
5 +	2 + 3	2 + 0 + 1 + 9 =	22	2 + 2 = 4	APRIL 2020

IF YOU WERE BORN		AND THE YEAR IS	YOUR PERSONAL YEAR IS		AND IT RUNS
OCTOBER	15	2019		1 + 9 = 10	OCTOBER 2019
1 + 0 +	1 + 5	2 + 0 + 1 + 9 =	19	1 + 0 = 1	SEPTEMBER 2020

Your previous Personal Year number, which is active before your month of birth in any given calendar year, is one digit lower than the current year's (unless the current year's is a 1, in which case the previous year's was a 9).

Once you calculate your current yearly cycle, you can look back at previous personal years and forward to coming personal year cycles to gauge how these cycles have impacted you in the past and will impact you moving forward.

How to Calculate Your Personal MONTHS

Your Personal Months change at the beginning of each month. To find your Personal Months number, add the number of the month in question to your single-digit personal year number.

In the example above, the person born on May 23 calculated a 4 Personal Year in 2019. That means that her months are:

PERSONAL YEAR NUMBER	MONTH	PERSONAL MONTH NUMBER	
4 +	(MAY) 5	= 9	
4 +	(JUNE) 6	= 10	1 + 0 = 1
4 +	(JULY) 7	= 11	1 + 1 = 2
4 +	(AUGUST) 8	= 12	1 + 2 = 3
4 +	(SEPTEMBER) 9	= 13	1 + 3 = 4
4 +	(OCTOBER) 10	= 14	1 + 4 = 5
4 +	(NOVEMBER) 11	= 15	1 + 5 = 6
4 +	(DECEMBER) 12	= 16	1 + 6 = 7
4 +	(JANUARY 2020) 1	= 5	
4 +	(FEBRUARY) 2	= 6	
4 +	(MARCH) 3	= 7	
4 +	(APRIL) 4	= 8	

Note: September is the 9th month. Thus in September every year, your Personal Month number is the same as your Personal Year number. This is because adding 9 to any number and reducing the total sum to a single digit, results in the same number that you originally added to 9.

In the other example above, the person born on October 15 calculated a 1 Personal Year in 2019, beginning a brand new 9-year cycle. That means that her months are:

PERSONAL YEAR NUMBER	MONTH	PERSONAL MONTH NUMBER	
1 +	(OCTOBER) 10	= 11	1 + 1 = 2
1 +	(NOVEMBER) 11	= 12	1 = 2 = 3
1 +	(DECEMBER) 12	= 13	1 + 3 = 4
1 +	(JANUARY 2020) 1	= 2	
1 +	(FEBRUARY) 2	= 3	
1 +	(MARCH) 3	= 4	
1 +	(APRIL) 4	= 5	
1 +	(MAY) 5	= 6	
1 +	(JUNE) 6	= 7	
1 +	(JULY) 7	= 8	
1 +	(AUGUST) 8	= 9	
1 +	(SEPTEMBER) 9	= 10	

How to Calculate Your Personal DAYS

Take the Personal MONTH Number in question and add it to the DAY in question.

Personal Month __ + Day = __ Personal Day

For example, to find the Personal Day on May 6, 2019 for the person born on May 23:

PERSONAL MONTH NUMBER	DAY OF THE MONTH	PERSONAL DAY NUMBER
9 +	6	= 15 (1 + 5) = **6**

Read the descriptions for 4, the Personal Year Number, 9, the Personal Month Number, and 6, the Personal Day Number, in the Personal Cycles in Chapter 7.

To find this person's Personal Day for **September 29, 2019**:

PERSONAL MONTH NUMBER	DAY OF THE MONTH	PERSONAL DAY NUMBER
4 +	29 (2 + 9)	= 15 (1 + 5) = **6**

(continued)

Read the descriptions for 4 and 6 Personal Cycles in Chapter 7.

To find this person's Personal Day for **February 14, 2020**:

PERSONAL MONTH NUMBER	DAY OF THE MONTH	PERSONAL DAY NUMBER
6 +	14 (1 + 4)	= 11 (1 + 1) = **2**

Read the descriptions for 4, 6, and 2 Personal Cycles in Chapter 7.

As previously calculated, the person born on October 15 will enter a **1** Personal Year in October 2019, beginning a brand new 9-year cycle!

To find the Personal Month for **October 7, 2019**:

PERSONAL MONTH NUMBER	DAY OF THE MONTH	PERSONAL DAY NUMBER
2 +	7	= **9**

Read the descriptions for 1, 2, and 9 Personal Cycles in Chapter 7.

To find the Personal Month for **August 26, 2020**:

PERSONAL MONTH NUMBER	DAY OF THE MONTH	PERSONAL DAY NUMBER
9 +	26 (2 + 6)	= 17 (1 + 7) = **8**

Read the descriptions for 1, 9, and 8 Personal Cycles in Chapter 7.

To find the Personal Month for **September 30, 2020**:

PERSONAL MONTH NUMBER	DAY OF THE MONTH	PERSONAL DAY NUMBER
1 +	30 (3 + 1)	= **4**

Read the descriptions for 1 and 4 Personal Cycles in Chapter 7.

Your Power Cycles

There are certain Personal Years, Months and Days that activate one of the numbers in your Three Important Birth Numbers. When this happens you will feel an intensification of energy. You'll experience profound growth and more opportunities. These are your Power Cycles, and their enhancement happens *any time a current personal cycle number aligns with one of the numbers in your Soul Birth Blueprint.*

For example, if your Three Important Birth Numbers are 3, 7, and 4 (Day of Birth, Life Purpose, and Destiny), you want to note any Personal Year, Month, or Day that ALSO resonates to 3, 7, or 4. So, if you are experiencing a 4 Personal Year, Month or Day, you are activating your 4 Destiny Number. Make a note of these upcoming Power Cycles! Knowing about them will help you navigate your life with confidence and ease. You'll be able to leverage the profound vibrational alignment that place each and every time.

Keep in mind, you have several Power Cycle Personal Days each and every month—no matter whether you are in a Power Cycle Personal Month and Year—or not! So you are never without this surge of energy.

You have some Days and Months where two of your Three Important Birth Numbers are activated. This happens when a Personal Year and a Personal Day both align with one of your Three Important Birth Numbers at the same time. Or, it can be a Personal Month and Personal Day.

Once in a while, if your Personal Year and Personal Month both activate one of your Three Important Birth Numbers, you will have *triple intensification* Power Cycle days! That is when the Personal Year, Personal Month and Personal Day ALL resonate to one of the Three Important Numbers in your Birth Soul Blueprint.

Take advantage of any Power Cycle activation. It is a green light from the Universe to your Soul, letting you know—all systems go! Whatever you experience during these Year, Month or Day Power Cycles, it is designed to up your game, lift you higher and put you in greater touch with the Light of God—your Spiritual Source.

Now let's discover the meaning of your Personal Cycles!

CHAPTER 7

THE MEANING OF YOUR PERSONAL CYCLES

NOW THAT YOU KNOW HOW TO CALCULATE YOUR **PERSONAL YEARS,** Months, and Days as well as decipher when your Power Cycles are, it's time to give all the numbers meaning! You will discover how each number vibration, from 1 through 9, is activated. Use the interpretation for each number for all your cycles—year, month, and day.

BIRTH

9-Year Cycles

Every nine years you begin a new 9-year cycle, from Personal Year 1 through 9. Any time your 9-year cycle comes to an end (you are in a 9 Personal Year), or begins again (you are in a 1 Personal Year) you will feel a major shift in your life. You are releasing old paradigms and ways of being, people, and beliefs to make room for a rebirth.

This "shift" also happens to a lesser degree when you transition from a 9 Personal Month to a 1 Personal Month, and even from a 9 Personal Day to a 1 Personal Day.

As a reminder, your current and future cycles are comprised of:

1. Your **Personal Year**—the vibration you are experiencing from one birthday to the next birthday

2. Your **Personal Month**—each calendar month carries a specific personal vibration for you

3. Your **Personal Day**—every day carries a specific personal vibration for you

Whenever a Personal Day, Month, or Year is the same as one of your Three Important Birth Numbers, the impact will intensify.

1 Personal Year/Month/Day

Keywords: New beginnings, Action, Change, New goals.

Learning new modalities, fresh energy, completely letting go of beliefs, things, people and investments that are not supporting you, boldness, courage, opportunity, rebirth—you are at a *Crossroads*.

Shadow Side: guard against stubborn resistance to change, not focusing on and planning your future

- You are experiencing a new beginning in some or all areas of your life.

- Seed new original ideas.

- 1 cycles initiate, so put your ideas and ambitions into action.

- You are rebranding your life and thinking about yourself and your plans in refreshing new ways.

- This is an intense period of awakening.

- Your confidence is growing and making room for you to open up and explore bold new directions.

- Pay meticulous attention to new opportunities.

- Sudden change shifts you to the core.

- Fearlessly embrace and proclaim what makes you unique.

- Create and invent.

2 Personal Year/Month/Day

Keywords: Co-operation, New Partnerships (personal and business), Balance, Patience, Peace.

Relationships, diplomacy, slow down, meticulous attention to details, correct timing, trust that your goals are being taken care of, listening, intuition, germination of seeds planted during last cycle.

Shadow Side: guard against impatience, division, feeling insecure about making decisions.

- Your 2 cycle is bringing you into equilibrium—you must balance light and dark and embrace all of life.

- Listen to your inner voice for spiritual insights

- You are deeply sensitive to everyone and everything.

- Trust in the correct timing of events, and be patient.

- Allow your heart to decide for you.

- Seek relationships that create balance in your life.

- Communicate your message with compassion and sensitivity.

- Take time for serenity—honor your sweetness and beauty.

- Embrace your Inner Psychic!

3 Personal Year/Month/Day

Keywords: Creative Self Expression, Being Social, Sharing Feelings, Pleasure, Connections.

Circle of Friends, express your inner voice, relax about having fun, enjoyment of the arts, find what makes you happy, travel, action, optimism, unexpected events (3 sits on a rocker).

Shadow side: guard against emotional drama, distractions, moodiness.

- Your creativity is being channeled through many sources and expresses itself through you. Tune in.

- Express your feelings openly and with vulnerability.

- Take great joy in finding what fulfills you to the core of your being.

- Your imagination has no bounds!

- Staying Positive attracts many opportunities.

- Opportunities are seized with bold action.

- Share your vision through writing, speaking, art, dance, or music.

- Connect socially with others, especially your soul sisters and brothers.

- What moves you to tears? Follow that thread...

4 Personal Year/Month/Day

Keywords: Organization, Planning, Work, Take Care of Details, Concentration.

Very busy, use logic, manifest ideas step-by-step, security, home, perseverance, focus, commitment, accomplishment, laying a foundation as a preparation for the next cycle.

Shadow side: guard against working too hard, not relaxing, escaping responsibilities

- Dedicate this cycle to making your gifts real and tangible.

- You feel at peace and secure when you set goals that align with your true values.

- Structure and organize your ideas and strategies into a coherent plan.

- Work diligently at implementing your goals and you'll reap rich rewards.

- Pay meticulous attention to details.

- Your brilliant insights are grounded in a strong foundation that leaves profound impact.

- Focus on Family and Home.

- Balance practical tasks with exploring your inner genius.

5 Personal Year/Month/Day

Keywords: Pivot Point, Decisions, Risk, Opportunity, Surprises

Change, movement, adventure, choices, expect the unexpected, make quick decisions, travel, be open to new ideas, take a chance, freedom, big shift in the middle of your 9-year cycle.

Shadow side: guard against scattered energy, multi-tasking, not following through, restlessness, impatience

- Embrace change as a constant in your life.

- Freedom is the keyword for you this cycle.
  Be as flexible as possible!

- The element of Movement is very strong.

- Abundance responds to fast action.

- You are transforming your life by taking a risk that takes you beyond your wildest dreams.

- Exploration is your ticket to independence and fulfillment.

- You will be faced with many large and small decisions. Make them quickly, so your energy does not stagnate.

- Travel to unknown realms—physically and mentally, and welcome all breakthroughs.

- Connect with others, share your new ideas.

6 Personal Year/Month/Day

Keywords: Taking on responsibilities, Family, Love, Home, Relationships, Home business, Wealth

Health, house, harmony, compassion, beauty in your environment, helping others, emotional, personal growth, connecting to close friends, birth of new opportunities, emotional equilibrium

Shadow side: guard against neglecting your needs, taking on too much responsibility, emotional imbalance

- Embrace your responsibilities fully and with joy.

- Be open to heal yourself and you will be a healing influence on others.

- Explore empathy and embrace being of loving service.

- Your passion for life, and compassion for others is expanded in this cycle.

- Focus on financial expansion and wealth.

- Make your life and surroundings exquisitely beautiful—listen to beautiful music.

- Attend to your health and bodily well-being.

- Nurture yourself—you are giving a lot this cycle and must replenish.

- You are birthing a new way to succeed, inspired to thrive on your terms, not in servitude to another or outside expectations.

- Seek all fulfillment through love.

- Focus on home and family.

7 Personal Year/Month/Day

Keywords: Lightning Spiritual Insights, Intuition, Let Go and Let God, Sudden Discoveries

Sabbatical, wisdom, learn and take a class, introspection, slow down, recognition, honor, spend time in nature, plan, seek rejuvenation, read books, expect the unexpected, spend time by yourself.

Shadow side: guard against analyzing, over-thinking, worrying and doubting

- Listen and act on strong intuitive insights.

- Fulfillment comes by both thinking through your plans and implementing your brilliant ideas.

- Embrace sudden shifts as opportunities for growth.

- Your wisdom expands exponentially through deep learning and understanding.

- Be a bridge between spiritual and material realms.

- Realize your intuitions and visions by taking time for retreats and relaxation.

- Trust your hunches.

- Seek wisdom and truth.

- Rest.

8 Personal Year/Month/Day

Keywords: Focus on Money, Goals, Strength, Manifest your Power, Energy expended = Rewards

Money matters, take action, balance material and spiritual, focus energy, gain strength by overcoming obstacles, prosperity, rewards, honors, ambition, be efficient and practical.

Shadow side: guard against fear of success, doubt of own power to succeed, inability to follow through on goals

- This is your cycle of empowerment.

- You are very motivated to manifest.

- You exude confidence in everything you do, think and envision about your future.

- Lead and you will succeed.

- A strong focus on finances affects the impact of your vision.

- You are motivated to fulfill your destiny.

- Overcoming obstacles makes you stronger.

- The energy you expend enriches you and brings rewards.

9 Personal Year/Month/Day

Keywords: Completion, Culmination, Celebration, Release, Endings

Finish what you began 8 years ago, be of service, compassion, release beliefs and people who are keeping you stuck in old behaviors, feng-shui your life, a testing year of courage and strength, endings.

Shadow side: guard against feeling discouraged and dissipated emotionally, resisting the urge to let go

- Embrace endings and celebrate your successes.

- Leading from a place of love creates deep fulfillment.

- Release ideas, beliefs, things, people that you've outgrown or do not support or uplift you

- Complete all projects by the end of this cycle to reap rewards.

- By being a wise example to others, your love instills courage.

- Embrace all life has to offer—both challenges and joyful events—for the greatest abundance.

- Letting go of values acquired from others (and mistakenly attributed as your own) opens up miraculous doors.

- You have come to the end of a cycle and are making room for a rebirth.

CHAPTER 8

ADDRESS NUMBERS

JUST AS EVERY PERSON EMITS A SPECIAL CODE, EACH ADDRESS CARRIES A SPECIFIC VIBRATION. There are three important items you need to know about your address number:

1. Is it an overall fortunate vibration?

2. If yes, does the vibration resonate with one of your three important birth numbers?

3. If not, what remedy can you use to introduce a secondary positive influence?

Address numbers have different effects on your life, so it is important to understand how your address affects you, whether it is your personal address or business address. This knowledge alone will have a major effect on your daily life. You'll be able to know which addresses keep you in the flow, with minimal challenging interference and distractions—and just as importantly, which do not.

HOW TO CALCULATE ANY ADDRESS

In any address that impacts your life, only the number is important to you. You do not need to calculate the street name. The only instance where a letter will be considered as part of the calculation process is when a letter appears in your actual address number, such as 555 Cedar St., #**9H**.

Let's look at variations of addresses you may encounter in your life:

First write down the number of your address.

1. For a simple street address, without an apartment number, simply write down the number.

If you live at 4816 Main St., write down **4816**.
Add all the numbers until you can bring the total down to a single digit "root" number:

4816 $= 4 + 8 + 1 + 6 =$ **19**
19 $= 1 + 9 =$ **10**
10 $= 1 + 0 =$ **1**

The address number for this property is **1.**

2. If you live in an apartment or condo, you must calculate both the street number of your whole building AND the unit number of your condo *separately.* Your building number is of lesser importance than the unit number—since only the unit number is unique to *you.* The unit number is your personal address vibration.

For 4816 Main St., **#25**
25 = 2 + 5 = **7**

The address number for this unit is 7. We already know that 4816 Main St. adds up to a "root" number of 1. But **7**, the unit number, *has the greatest influence on the inhabitant(s).* Number 1 for 4816 Main St. has a secondary impact.

3. For addresses with letters you must add the numeric value for the letter *with AND without the equivalent number value of the letter.*

An address of 32 Apple Dr. #8B would be added:

8 + **B** = **8 + 2** = 10
10 = 1 + 0 = **1**
Without the Letter B this address ALSO vibrates to number 8.

So this condo unit activates **both the numbers 1 and 8.**

It is important to calculate BOTH versions—with and without the letter whenever a number and letter are present. Thus, *look at the number as a standalone vibration and the total of the number and letter.*

1	2	3	4	5	6	7	8	9
A	B	C	D	E	F	G	H	I
J	K	L	M	N	O	P	Q	R
S	T	U	V	W	X	Y	Z	

HOW YOUR ADDRESS ALIGNS WITH YOUR BIRTH CODE

Look at all the single digits that make up your Three Important Birth Numbers (Chapters 1 & 2).

Figure out which of the three Triads they resonate to (Chapter 3).

If ONE of your Three Important Birth Numbers is activated by your single digit address number, your address number will resonate with you. However, you still need to check if your address activates a "challenging" vibration. Even if it resonates with you, it may attract challenges if it is not connected to abundance.

Meaning of Your Address

Remember, as long as ONE of your Three Important Birth Numbers resonates with the single digit of your address, you are compatible with the address.

1 ADDRESSES / UNIT NUMBERS:

- Optimism, achievement and manifesting new ideas.

- If you're looking for a fresh start a number 1 address gives you the confidence and strength.

- Good for those who are self-employed or want to live alone and/or work alone.

- Favors activation and determination, not a laid-back lifestyle.

- 1 addresses do not like any clutter. 1 thrives on clarity and cleanliness.

- A 1 address is good for people who are naturally independent—though favors partners who are inter-dependent, and respect each others personal freedom and boundaries.

  Great for Birth Code Numbers **1, 5,** and **7**.
  Good for Birth Code Numbers **3, 8,** and **9**.
  Not recommended for Birth Code Numbers **2, 4,** and **6**.

2 ADDRESSES / UNIT NUMBERS:

- **2 addresses** favor partnerships and love (please see exceptions in next section).

- 2 addresses foster harmony and balance.

- 2 is more laid-back and not as connected to manifesting financial abundance.

- Putting career first is not as easy—relating with compassion and consideration are the major themes.

- You can feel more emotional and co-dependent in a 2 address.

- Favors meditation and diplomacy in a compassionate, nurturing environment.

- Getting caught up in other people's life and feelings is something to be aware of.

- 2 addresses are wonderful for sharing, settling down with a family and having roommates.

  Great for Birth Code Numbers **2, 4,** and **8**.
  Good for Birth Code Numbers **3, 6,** and **9**.
  Not recommended for Birth Code Numbers **1, 5,** and **7**.

- ** Avoid addresses that initially add up to 11, 29, 38, or 47. Addresses that add are **2** or **20** are good.

3 ADDRESSES / UNIT NUMBERS:

- **3 addresses** are perfect for the creative, free-spirited person.

- 3 homes attract movement, activity, emotional expression and change

- 3 can scatter energy and does not plan for the future, so this address is less likely to attract financial abundance.

- 3 homes foster communication and social engagement.

- 3 addresses attract optimism, fun and are great for parties and social gatherings.

- 3 addresses activate your imagination.

- In a 3 address, being clean and tidy is not a priority.

- 3 invites sharing and emotional self expression—not practical, serious endeavors.

  Great for Birth Code Numbers **3, 6,** and **9**.
  Good for Birth Code Numbers **1, 2,** and **5**.
  Not recommended for Birth Code Numbers **4, 7,** and **8**.

** *Avoid addresses that initially add up to 12, 39, or 48. Addresses that add are **3, 21,** or **30** are good.*

4 ADDRESSES / UNIT NUMBERS:

- **4 addresses** bring a sense of order, stability and long-term residents.

- 4 addresses foster slow and steady progress and protection.

- 4 is the number of diligent work, so this space won't be as relaxing.

- 4 addresses do not support freedom or a flowing sense of ease.

- 4 addresses are more serious than fun.

- A 4 address is not as aligned with generating financial abundance.

- In a 4 house you'll need to be patient and know that manifestation will take effort.

- A 4 address is good for study, work, security, and stability. Structure, order, and discipline influence this address.

  Good for Birth Code Numbers **2**, **6**, and **7**.
  Not recommended for Birth Code Numbers **3, 4, 5, 8,** and **9**.

- ** *4 addresses in general are best avoided, since they make it more challenging to attract abundance.*

Note: *Any person with a **4** or **8 Day of Birth** or **4** or **8 Life Purpose Number** should **not** live in a **4** address. (This rule does not apply if your Destiny Number reduces to 4 or 8.)*

5 ADDRESSES / UNIT NUMBERS:

- **5 addresses** are very active energetically, inviting exploration and risk, not peace and quiet.

- A 5 home favors communication, media and connection with people.

- Traveling, adventure, pleasure and freedom are magnified in a 5 address.

- Any excessive behavior or addiction is amplified in a 5 home.

- 5 addresses favor variety and don't tend to be permanent residences.

- Amplifies fearlessness and progressive ideas—living life to the fullest.

- Your curiosity is piqued and new exciting experiences are welcomed.

- People come and go in 5 addresses—they have a sense of unpredictability.

   Great for Birth Code Numbers **1, 5,** and **7**.
   Good for Birth Code Numbers **3** and **9**.
   Not recommended for Birth Code Numbers **2, 4, 6,** and **8**.

6 ADDRESSES / UNIT NUMBERS:

- **6 addresses** radiate with warmth, cheer, beauty and compassion.

- A 6 address is a wonderful family home and favors love and abundance.

- Your creativity and inspiration are magnified at a 6 address.

- People of all ages can reside here and feel nurtured and cared for.

- 6 addresses invoke strong responsibilities so keep the balance with self-care in order not to get drained energetically.

- A 6 address favors running a home business and any endeavors related to providing a service.

- The focus is on acceptance, trust and building strong family bonds.

- A 6 address can be a beautiful sanctuary for the heart and soul.

Great for Birth Code Numbers **3, 6,** and **9**.
Good for Birth Code Numbers **2, 4,** and **8**.
Not recommended for Birth Code Numbers **1, 5,** and **7**.

7 ADDRESSES / UNIT NUMBERS:

- **7 addresses** are peaceful, meditative, spiritual, and favor personal development.

- Favors learning, studying philosophy, esoteric subjects, and all education.

- This is a private, quiet address—a refuge—noise must be kept to a minimum to not disturb the peace.

- At times, sudden events bring deep transformation.

- 7 addresses are more suited for the single person, not families or couples.

- Solitude, contemplation, intellectual pursuits, intense devotion, and a connection to nature are favored.

- This address is not recommended for manifesting financial abundance.

- Escape everyday stresses in this retreat home—favors writers, healers, spiritual seekers.

   Great for Birth Code Numbers **1, 5,** and **7**.
   Good for Birth Code Numbers **4**.
   Not recommended for Birth Code Numbers **2, 3, 6, 8,** and **9**.

** *Avoid addresses that initially add up to 16, 25, 34, or 43. Addresses that add to **7** are good, if you don't mind that this property won't be a major abundance attractor.*

8 ADDRESSES / UNIT NUMBERS:

- **8 addresses** favor leadership, power, success, and a strong focus on manifesting money.

- Favors running a home business, but not necessarily family life.

- Helps you to be recognized for your mission, expertise, career.

- 8 addresses must exude elegance with quality furniture and luxury items.

- 8 addresses do not encourage social events or casual visitors.

- Favors manifesting financial abundance, organization, endurance, overcoming obstacles, and management.

- This address is about prestige and power.

- Keep a balance on spiritual and physical fulfillment.

  Great for Birth Code Numbers **2**.
  Good for Birth Code Numbers **1, 5**, and **6**.
  Not recommended for Birth Code Numbers **3, 4, 7, 8,** and **9**.

  Note: *Any person with a **4** or **8 Day of Birth** or **4** or **8 Life Purpose Number** should **not** live in a **4** address. (This rule does not apply if your Destiny Number reduces to 4 or 8.)*

** Avoid addresses that initially add up to 26, 35, or 44. Addresses that add are **8** or **17** are good.

9 ADDRESSES / UNIT NUMBERS:

- **9 addresses** favor spiritual leadership, empathy, unconditional love, teaching, and family.

- Favors settling down long-term, completion of goals, and love.

- Supports interaction with extended family and friends.

- 9 addresses exude warmth, tolerance, compassion, and acceptance of all.

- 9 addresses favor creativity and inspirational pursuits.

- In a 9 space you want to make the world a better place and give something back.

- Supports abundance generation and spiritual growth.

- Living here will put the focus on letting go, seeking higher wisdom, forgiveness, and giving.

    Great for Birth Code Numbers **3, 6,** and **9**.
    Good for Birth Code Numbers **1, 2,** and **5**.
    Not recommended for Birth Code Numbers **4, 7,** and **8**.

** Avoid addresses that initially add up to 18. Addresses that add are **9, 27,** or **36** are good.

Remedies for Challenging Address Numbers

(And How to Align These to Your Soul Birth Code)

If an address number is either challenging or not in harmony with one of your birth numbers there is an easy remedy to diminish a challenging address and infuse it with a secondary positive vibration.

Place a number inside the front door (anywhere on the door, but it must be *inside the main door* of the residence or office—thus facing into the home.

This number is added to the single digit address number.

Make sure the new digit double digit and single digit address number resonates with one of the Three Important Numbers in your Birth Code.

Make sure the number is positive and is not listed in the "Avoid" section.

For example, if you live in a 12 home (which is in the "Avoid" section under 3 addresses), you want to add the root number 3 (12 = 1 + 2 = 3) to a single digit for which the new sum reduces to a number that supports you.

Let's say you would like to add a secondary positive vibration that reduces to **6**. Add a **3** to the existing 3 (3 + 3 = 6). **Place a 3 inside the front door** to your home or office or condo and start benefitting from a fortunate secondary influence of a 6 address in your life.

Keep in mind, the dominant address vibration will still be 12 (which reduces to 3). However now you have diluted the influence of this challenging address number by placing a 3 inside the front door, thus creating a NEW secondary positive influence of number 6.

ACKNOWLEDGMENTS

I would like to acknowledge the support and inspiration of my daughter Clara, whose love of numerology, astrology and music and thirst for wisdom have brought infinite joy into my life each and every day.

I thank Pythagoras, the great philosopher, musician, mathematician, numerologist, astronomer and astrologer, and subject of the first book on numerology I pulled off a bookshelf in a spiritual bookstore in Amherst, Massachusetts, while I was a student at the college. This book featured Pythagoras' spiritual teachings on numerology and changed my life.

Thank you to my father for introducing me to astrology as a teenager—his love of all things spiritual and the hidden nature of life still fuels my quest for wisdom to this day.

So much gratitude to my wonderful core team—Nancy, AJ, and Jelena—for your dedication and patience during the book creation process. Also to Angela, Heidii, and Paula for your continual work and support. It is because of you that the powerful message in the stars and numbers continues to expand and uplift!

Big thank you to Jill Alexander for your support and encouragement!

Finally, to all my students and clients—I've learned so much from you and appreciate your trust and support! It has been a profound honor to share and teach the wonderful world of star codes over these many years, and I hope you find this handbook as much of a delight to read and apply as it has been to write!

ABOUT THE AUTHOR

Wealth Astro-Numerologist and Psychic Tania Gabrielle introduced the merging of two ancient divination arts— Astrology and Numerology—to the Western World. Renowned as a gifted channel, Tania unlocks the codes in the stars, names and numbers to facilitate wealth and well-being. In decoding each person's birth promise and forecast map, Tania guides her clients to claim their true destiny and divine mission. Her primary focus is on teaching spiritual principles that manifest practical, real-life results.

Tania was featured and quoted in *The New York Times*, *Los Angeles Times, USA Today, Entertainment Weekly, ESPN Magazine, Essence Magazine, ESPN.com*, *Yahoo. com*, and *US Magazine.* She has appeared as an excerpt in two documentaries—*Quantum Communication* and *The Voice.* Tania is also a gifted classical composer, with her music performed worldwide in the most prestigious concert halls by Grammy-award-winning artists.

As founder and creator of *Numerology Academy*, the first online certification course in Astro-Numerology, Tania continues to guide thousands of students around the globe who, in turn, help others to create extraordinary lives.

Visit her at TaniaGabrielle.com.

INDEX

Addiction, 56, 163
Address numbers, 155–169
Adoption, 21
Affection/being affectionate, 40, 43, 57, 125
Affirmations
    Root Number 1, 42
    for Root Number 2 people, 47
    for Root Number 3 people, 51
    for Root Number 4 people, 53
    for Root Number 5 people, 57
    for Root Number 6 people, 59
    for Root Number 7 people, 63
    for Root Number 8 people, 66–67
    for Root Number 9 people, 69
Analytical traits, 34, 60
Anxiety/being anxious, 98, 110, 124
Apartment, Address Number and, 157
Art(s) and aesthetics, 58, 74, 81, 92
Astrology, 36, 131

Balance, 42, 73, 145
Birth Certificate name. See Destiny Number
Birth Code, 9–17. See also Destiny Number
    about, 9
    Address Numbers and, 158–167
    case studies, 23–41
    Day of Birth Number, 10, 11–13
    Life Purpose Number, 10, 14–17
    numerology triads, 34–36, 39
    Power Cycles and, 138
Birthday, Personal Year number beginning on your, 131
Blueprint of your Soul, 9, 130, 138, 139
Business, 64, 97, 109, 113, 119

Calculations
    of address number, 156–157
    for your Birth Number, 11–14
    for your Destiny Number, 21–31
    for your Life Purpose Number, 15–17
    for your Personal Day, 135–137
    for your Personal Month, 133–134
    for your Personal Year, 130–132
Career, Destiny Number and, 19–20, 24, 26, 28, 30

Case studies
    Destiny Number, 23–31
    Life Purpose Number, 16–17
Challenging address numbers, remedying, 168–169
Challenging expressions. See also Shadow side
    for Root Number 1 people, 41
    for Root Number 2 people, 44–46
    for Root Number 3 people, 49–51
    for Root Number 4 people, 52–53
    for Root Number 5 people, 56–57
    for Root Number 6 people, 58–59
    for Root Number 7 people, 62–63
    for Root Number 8 people, 66
    for Root Number 9 people, 68–69
Change, 55, 56, 60, 83–84, 91, 94, 104, 107, 118, 125, 144, 148
Co-dependence, 43
Compassion, 35, 37, 47, 52, 57, 67, 79–80, 116, 119, 120, 122, 126, 127, 149, 160
Compound Life Purpose Number, 15–17
Condominium, Address Number and, 157
Conformity, 78
Cosmic Guardian, Master Number 33, 79–81
"Creation" Triad, 35–36
Creativity/creative expression, 35, 47, 49, 51, 58, 61, 73, 81, 84, 94, 95, 99, 107, 113, 115, 117, 121, 125, 146, 164, 167

Day of Birth Numbers
    about, 10, 11
    address numbers and, 162, 166
    calculating, 11–14
    calculating Personal Year number and, 132
    Destiny Number and, 20, 23–31
    numerical triads and, 39
    Power Cycles and, 138
Destiny Number
    about, 11, 19–20
    calculating your, 21–23
    case studies, 23–31
    as Master Number 55, 83
    as Master Number 66, 84
    as Master Number 88, 86
    as Master Number 99, 87
    reducing to 4 or 8, 162, 166

Details, attention to, 45, 51, 68, 145, 147
Double-digit numbers, 13. *See also*
  Master numbers; individual numbers
Double intelligence, 83, 85

Education, 49, 90, 165
Emotional self-expression, 161
Empathy, 79–80, 84
Enigma, 51, 68

Family and friends, 49, 52, 65, 114, 167
Feng-shui, 52, 152
Finances and money, 43–44, 60, 63–64,
  162. *See also* Money and money matters
Foreign letters, in Pythagorean system, 23
Freedom, 47, 53–55, 95, 100, 105, 107, 108,
  109, 110, 114, 148
Freedom Seeker, Master Number 55 and,
  83–84

Group consciousness, 81

Helping others, 37, 67–68, 81, 87, 92, 120,
  122, 124, 149
Hemingway, Mariel, 16, 25–26
Home business, 164, 166
Home/house, 45, 52, 58, 104, 122, 125, 149

Ideals and idealism, 48, 67, 82, 96, 109,
  110, 117, 126, 127
Illusion, 73, 75, 77
Imagination, 40, 42–43, 44, 67, 82, 91, 108,
  146, 161
Impatience, 68, 91, 92
Independence, 40, 47, 48, 49, 78, 101, 105,
  106, 126, 159
Inner voice, 73, 74, 118, 145, 146
Insecurity, 94, 95
Intelligence/intellect, 34, 40, 52, 53, 61,
  64, 83, 85, 95, 108, 110, 112, 113, 114,
  119, 127
Intensifications, 27, 33, 39, 139. *See also*
  Master numbers
Intuition, 10, 34, 43, 44, 52, 61, 81, 84, 92,
  102, 105, 106, 115, 116, 119, 121, 125,
  150
Intuitive Master, Master Number 11 and,
  73–76

King, Martin Luther, Jr., 17, 29–31

Leadership, 20, 39, 63, 65, 67–68, 73,
  81–82, 86, 87, 93, 97, 98, 109, 115, 119,
  120, 121, 122, 123, 127
Learning, 34
Letters, Destiny Number and, 21–31
Life Purpose Number, 10, 14–17, 20,
  24–30, 39, 162, 166

Managers, 42–43
Manifestation Triad, 34–35, 39, 43, 45
Master Number 11, 29, 73–76
Master Number 22, 76–78
Master Number 33, 79–81
Master Number 44, 81–83
Master Number 55, 83–84
Master Number 66, 84–85
Master Number 77, 85
Master Number 88, 85
Master Number 99, 87
Master numbers, 71
Maya, 75
"Mind" Triad, 34
Money and money matters, 52, 58, 59,
  64, 83, 97, 103, 114, 151, 166. *See also*
  Finances and money

Nature, 20, 61, 115, 127
New beginnings, 144
9-year cycles, 143–152
Number 0, 37
Number 1
    addresses/unit numbers, 159
    Personal Year/Month/Day, 144
    Root Number 1, 39–42
Number 2
    addresses/unit numbers, 160
    Destiny Number, 26
    Personal Year/Month/Day, 145
    Root Number 2, 42–46
Number 3
    addresses/unit numbers, 161
    Day of Life Number, 20
    Destiny Number and, 20
    Personal Year/Month/Day, 146
    Root Number 3 people, 49–51
Number 4
    addresses/unit numbers, 162
    Day of Birth Number, 24, 25
    Personal Year/Month/Day, 147
    Root Number 4, 51–53
Number 5
    addresses/unit numbers, 163
    Life Purpose Number, 25

Personal Year/Month/Day, 148
Root Number 5 people, 53–57
Number 6
    addresses/unit numbers, 164
    Life Purpose Number, 24
    Personal Year/Month/Day, 149
    Root Number 6 people, 57–59
Number 7
    addresses/unit numbers, 165
    Personal Year/Month/Day, 150
    Root Number 7 people, 60–63
Number 8
    addresses/unit numbers, 166
    Destiny Number, 20, 24, 28
    Personal Year/Month/Day, 151
    Root Number 8 people, 63–66
Number 9
    addresses/unit numbers, 167
    Personal Year/Month/Day, 152
    Root Number 9 people, 67–69
Number 10, 90
Number 11. See Master Number 11
Number 11/2, 14, 27, 28, 30
Number 12, 90
Number 13, 91
Number 14, 91
Number 15, 92
Number 16, 92
Number 17, 93
Number 18, 93
Number 19, 15, 94
Number 20, 93
Number 21, 95
Number 22. See Master Number 22
Number 23, 95
Number 24, 96
Number 25, 96
Number 26, 97
Number 27, 97
Number 28, 15, 98
Number 29, 15, 98
Number 30, 99
Number 31, 99
Number 32, 100
Number 33. See Master Number 33
Number 34, 100
Number 35, 101
Number 36, 101
Number 37, 15, 102
Number 38, 15, 102
Number 39, 15, 103
Number 40, 103
Number 41, 104

Number 42, 104
Number 43, 105
Number 44. See Master Number 44
Number 45, 105
Number 46, 15, 106
Number 47, 15, 106
Number 48, 15, 107
Number 49, 107
Number 50, 108
Number 51, 108
Number 52, 109
Number 53, 109
Number 54, 110
Number 55. See Master Number 55
Number 56, 110
Number 57, 110
Number 58, 111
Number 59, 111
Number 60, 112
Number 61, 112
Number 62, 113
Number 63, 113
Number 64, 113–114
Number 65, 114
Number 66. See Master Number 66
Number 67, 114
Number 68, 115
Number 69, 115
Number 70, 115–116
Number 71, 116
Number 72, 116
Number 73, 117
Number 74, 117
Number 75, 117–118
Number 76, 118
Number 77. See Master Number 77
Number 78, 118
Number 79, 119
Number 80, 119
Number 81, 120
Number 82, 120
Number 83, 121
Number 84, 121
Number 85, 121–122
Number 86, 122
Number 87, 122
Number 88. See Master Number 88
Number 89, 123
Number 90, 123
Number 91, 124
Number 92, 124
Number 93, 125
Number 94, 125

Number 95, 126
Number 96, 126
Number 97, 127
Number 98, 127
Number 99. *See* Master Number 99

1-5-7 "Mind" Triad, 34
Organizational skills, 51, 64
Out-of-the-box thinking, 91, 99, 124

Patience, 42, 64, 145
Peace, Master Architect of, 76–78
Peace/peacemaker, 42, 93, 102, 103, 111,
  124, 145, 165
Perfectionism, 59, 62, 68, 80, 97, 98
Personal Cycles
        9-year cycles, 143–152
        Personal Days, 135–137
        Personal Month, 133–134
        Personal Year, 130–133
        Power Cycles and, 130, 138–139
Power Cycles, 130, 138–139
Psychic abilities, 43, 67, 85, 117
Pythagorean (Western) Numerology
  Alphabet system, 21–23

Relationships, 43, 56, 61, 62, 68, 77, 97, 99,
  102, 145
Robbins, Tony, 17, 27–28
Romance, 43, 57
Root Life Purpose Number, 15–17
Root number(s)
        address numbers and, 168
        calculating Day of Birth, 13–14
        Destiny Number and, 20, 22
        Root Number 1 people, 39–41
        Root Number 2 people, 42–46
        Root Number 3 career environment,
          20
        Root Number 3 people, 47–51
        Root Number 4 people, 51–53
        Root Number 5 people, 53–57
        Root Number 6 people, 57–59
        Root Number 7 career environment,
          20
        Root Number 7 people, 60–63
        Root Number 8 people, 63–66
        Root Number 9 people, 67–69

Secrecy, 43, 62
Self-employment, 159
Shadow side. *See also* Challenging
  expressions

of 8 Personal Year/Month Date, 151
of 5 Personal Year/Month Date, 148
of 4 Personal Year/Month Date, 147
of 9 Personal Year/Month Date, 152
of number 10, 90
of number 12, 90
of number 13, 91
of number 14, 91
of number 15, 92
of number 16, 92
of number 20, 94
of number 21, 95
of number 23, 95
of number 24, 96
of number 26, 97
of number 27, 97
of number 28, 98
of number 30, 99
of number 31, 99
of number 32, 100
of number 34, 100
of number 36, 101
of number 37, 102
of number 38, 102
of number 39, 103
of number 40, 103
of number 41, 104
of number 42, 104
of number 43, 105
of number 45, 105
of number 46, 106
of number 47, 106
of number 48, 107
of number 49, 107
of number 50, 108
of number 51, 108
of number 52, 109
of number 53, 109
of number 54, 110
of number 56, 110
of number 57, 110
of number 58, 111
of number 59, 111
of number 60, 112
of number 61, 112
of number 62, 113
of number 63, 113
of number 64, 114
of number 65, 114
of number 67, 114
of number 68, 115
of number 69, 115
of number 70, 116

of number 71, 116
of number 72, 116
of number 73, 117
of number 74, 117
of number 75, 118
of number 76, 118
of number 78, 118
of number 79, 119
of number 80, 119
of number 81, 120
of number 82, 120
of number 83, 121
of number 84, 121
of number 85, 122
of number 86, 122
of number 87, 122
of number 89, 123
of number 90, 123
of number 91, 124
of number 92, 124
of number 93, 125
of number 94, 125
of number 95, 126
of number 96, 126
of number 97, 128
of number 98, 127
of 1-5-7 "Mind" Triad people, 34
of 1 Personal Year/Month Date, 144
of 7 Personal Year/Month Date, 150
of 6 Personal Year/Month Date, 149
of 3-6-9 "Creation" Triad people, 36
of 3 Personal Year/Month Date, 146
of 22/4, 40
of 2-4-8 "Manifestation" Triad
    people, 34–35
of 2 Personal Year/Month Date, 145
Shyness, 43, 46, 63
Single digit numbers. See also Names of
individual numbers; Root number(s)
    1-5-7 "Mind" Triad, 34
    2-4-8 "Manifestation" Triad, 34
    3-6-9 "Creation" Triad, 35–36
    Life Purpose Number, 15
    Master Numbers and, 71
Solar Return astrology chart, 131
Soul Birth Blueprint, 138
Spiritual growth/leadership, 48, 54, 60, 64,
76–78, 84, 85, 96, 150, 165, 167
Suffixes, in birth names, 22

Temple of Awareness, 74
3-6-9 "Creation" Triad, 35–36, 81
Timberlake, Justin, 16, 23–24
Travel, 48, 55, 60, 107, 112, 123, 126, 148
Triads
    1-5-7 "Mind" Triad, 34
    2-4-8 "Manifestation" Triad, 34–35
    3-6-9 "Creation" Triad, 35–36
    Address Number and, 158
    grouping of Birth Code numbers
        in, 39
    learning about others through,
        36–37
Trinity of Mother-Father-Child, 47
Two-digit number, Life Purpose Number
and, 15. See also specific two-digit
numbers
2-4-8 "Manifestation" Triad, 34–35, 45

Unconditional love, 75, 79, 87, 126, 127
Universal Year number, 130–131

Visionary, 81–83, 108

Wisdom, 42, 60, 61, 62, 69, 87, 90, 98, 102,
119, 123, 125, 127, 150
Worry, 34, 41, 116, 150

Zero. See Number 0